Company's Coming®

simmering stews

Choice recipes from
Company's Coming cookbooks

Jean Paré

aromatic beef stew

Coriander, cumin, honey and mint—here's a taste of the casbah! Pair this with couscous to play up the North African theme. Snip the extra mint into a small bowl so guests can add it to their plates.

All-purpose flour	1/4 cup	60 mL
Stewing beef, trimmed of fat	2 lbs.	900 g
Cooking oil	2 tsp.	10 mL
Cooking oil	2 tsp.	10 mL
Chopped onion	2 cups	500 mL
Garlic cloves, minced (or 1/2 tsp., 2 mL, powder)	2	2
Dried crushed chilies	1 tsp.	5 mL
Ground coriander	1 tsp.	5 mL
Ground cumin	1 tsp.	5 mL
Ground ginger	1 tsp.	5 mL
Low-sodium prepared beef broth	1 1/2 cups	375 mL
Medium carrots, chopped	2	2
Chopped celery	3/4 cup	175 mL
Salt (optional)	1/4 tsp.	1 mL
Chopped fresh mint	1/4 cup	60 mL
Liquid honey	2 tbsp.	30 mL

Put flour into large resealable freezer bag. Add beef. Seal bag. Toss until coated. Remove beef.

Heat first amount of cooking oil in large saucepan or Dutch oven on medium. Cook beef in 2 batches, stirring occasionally, until browned. Transfer to plate. Set aside.

Heat second amount of cooking oil in same saucepan on medium. Add onion and garlic. Cook for 5 to 10 minutes, stirring often and scraping any brown bits from bottom of pan, until onion is softened.

Add next 4 ingredients. Heat and stir for 1 to 2 minutes until fragrant.

Add next 4 ingredients and beef. Stir. Bring to a boil. Reduce heat to medium-low. Simmer, covered, for about 1 1/2 hours until beef is tender. Simmer, uncovered, for 15 to 20 minutes until sauce is slightly thickened.

Add mint and honey. Heat and stir on medium until heated through. Makes about 5 cups (1.25 L). Serves 8.

1 serving: 192 Calories; 6.0 g Total Fat (2.8 g Mono, 0.9 g Poly, 1.4 g Sat); 44 mg Cholesterol; 15 g Carbohydrate; 2 g Fibre; 20 g Protein; 259 mg Sodium

roasted vegetable stew

If you want to make extra to freeze for a busy day, you can double the first part of the recipe (up to the cornstarch) and then remove half to store before continuing. Roasted veggies shouldn't be frozen—add them after you've thawed the meat.

Olive (or cooking) oil	1 tbsp.	15 mL
Stewing beef (or inside round steak, cubed)	1 1/2 lbs.	680 g
Garlic cloves, minced (or 3/4 tsp., 4 mL, powder)	3	3
Pepper	1/2 tsp.	2 mL
Water	2 cups	500 mL
Can of condensed beef broth	10 oz.	284 mL
Dried thyme	1 1/2 tsp.	7 mL
Bay leaf	1	1
Water	2 tbsp.	30 ml
Cornstarch	1 tbsp.	15 mL
Halved baby potatoes	2 cups	500 mL
Medium fresh white mushrooms	12	12
Small tomatoes, quartered	6	6
Small onions, cut lengthwise into quarters	3	3
Halved baby carrots	1 cup	250 mL
Medium red or yellow pepper, slivered	1	1
Balsamic vinegar	2 tbsp.	30 mL
Olive (or cooking) oil	2 tbsp.	30 mL

Heat olive oil in large saucepan or Dutch oven on medium. Cook beef in 2 batches, stirring occasionally, until browned. Add garlic and pepper. Heat and stir for about 1 minute until fragrant.

Add next 4 ingredients. Stir. Bring to a boil. Reduce heat to medium-low. Simmer, covered, for about 1 1/2 hours until beef is tender.

Stir second amount of water into cornstarch in small cup. Add to beef mixture. Heat and stir for 1 to 2 minutes until boiling and slightly thickened. Discard bay leaf.

Put next 6 ingredients on large greased baking sheet with sides. Drizzle with vinegar and second amount of olive oil. Toss until coated. Bake in 425°F (220°C) oven for 20 minutes. Broil on top rack in oven, turning frequently, until skins are blistered and blackened. Add to beef mixture. Stir gently. Makes about 4 cups (1 L).

1 cup (250 mL): 433 Calories; 16.9 g Total Fat (10.0 g Mono, 1.6 g Poly, 3.6 g Sat); 67 mg Cholesterol; 39 g Carbohydrate; 7g Fibre; 34 g Protein; 565 mg Sodium

bean stew

Perfect after a day on the slopes. Make it the evening before and pull it from the fridge to gently reheat. This stew also freezes beautifully.

Cooking oil	1 tbsp.	15 mL
Lean ground beef	1 1/2 lbs.	680 g
Chopped onion	2 cups	500 mL
Bacon slices, diced	6	6
Cans of condensed tomato soup (10 oz., 284 mL, each)	2	2
Cans of kidney beans, with liquid (14 oz., 398 mL, each)	2	2
Medium carrots, thinly sliced	5	5
Medium peeled potatoes, cubed	5	5
Salt	1 tsp.	5 mL
Pepper	1/2 tsp.	2 mL

Heat cooking oil in large frying pan on medium-high. Add next 3 ingredients. Scramble-fry for about 10 minutes until beef is no longer pink. Drain.

Combine remaining 6 ingredients in large saucepan. Add beef mixture. Stir. Bring to a boil. Reduce heat to medium-low. Simmer, covered, for about 1 1/4 hours until vegetables are tender. Makes about 12 cups (3 L).

1 cup (250 mL): 269 Calories; 8.6 g Total Fat (3.7 g Mono, 1.3 g Poly, 2.7 g Sat); 32 mg Cholesterol; 32 g Carbohydrate; 7 g Fibre; 17 g Protein; 912 mg Sodium

autumn stew

When cutting up stewing meat, use a knife with a flat blade. A serrated edge will only tear the meat.

Cooking oil	1 tbsp.	15 mL
Beef inside round (or blade or chuck) steak, trimmed of fat and cut in bite-sized pieces	2 lbs.	900 g
Water	4 cups	1 L
Beef bouillon powder	2 tbsp.	30 mL
Salt	1/2 tsp.	2 mL
Pepper	1/2 tsp.	2 mL
Cubed peeled potato	4 cups	1 L
Diced carrot	3 cups	750 mL
Coarsely chopped onion	2 cups	500 mL
Cubed yellow turnip (or rutabaga)	1 cup	250 mL
Water	1/4 cup	60 mL
All-purpose flour	2 tbsp.	30 mL
Light sour cream	1 cup	250 mL

Heat cooking oil in large saucepan or Dutch oven on medium-high. Cook beef in 2 batches, for about 5 minutes per batch, stirring occasionally, until browned.

Add next 4 ingredients. Stir. Bring to a boil. Reduce heat to medium-low. Simmer, covered, for about 1 3/4 hours until beef is tender.

Add next 4 ingredients. Stir. Bring to a boil. Reduce heat to medium-low. Simmer, covered, for about 25 minutes until vegetables are tender.

Stir water into flour in small cup until smooth. Add to beef mixture. Heat and stir until boiling and thickened. Remove from heat.

Stir in sour cream (see Tip, page 64). Makes about 10 cups (2.5 L). Serves 8.

1 serving: 293 Calories; 6.8 g Total Fat (3.3 g Mono, 0.9 g Poly, 3.8 g Sat); 55 mg Cholesterol; 27 g Carbohydrate; 3 g Fibre; 31 g Protein; 718 mg Sodium

porcupine meatball stew

Grains of rice stud these meatballs, giving them their name. Be sure to use extra-lean ground beef—this avoids excess fat as the meatballs cook right in the stew.

Large egg, fork-beaten	1	1
Fine dry bread crumbs	1/3 cup	75 mL
Finely chopped onion	1/4 cup	60 mL
Garlic clove, minced	1	1
(or 1/4 tsp., 1 mL, powder)		
Seasoned salt	1 tsp.	5 mL
Pepper	1/8 tsp.	0.5 mL
Extra-lean ground beef	1 lb.	454 g
Long grain white rice	1/4 cup	60 mL
Small onion, cut into 6 wedges	1	1
Medium peeled potatoes, cubed	2	2
Sliced carrot	2 1/4 cups	550 mL
Diced green pepper	1/2 cup	125 mL
Can of stewed tomatoes	14 oz.	398 mL
Water	1/2 cup	125 mL
Beef bouillon powder	1 tsp.	5 mL

Combine first 6 ingredients in medium bowl.

Add beef and rice. Mix well. Roll into 12 balls. Arrange in ungreased 3 quart (3 L) casserole.

Layer next 4 ingredients, in order given, over meatballs.

Combine remaining 3 ingredients in small saucepan. Bring to a boil. Pour over vegetables. Bake, covered, in 325°F (160°C) oven for about 2 hours until meatballs are fully cooked and internal temperature of beef reaches 160°F (71°C). Makes about 6 cups (1.5 L). Serves 4.

1 serving: 558 Calories; 18.3 g Total Fat (7.7 g Mono, 1.2 g Poly, 6.9 g Sat); 146 mg Cholesterol; 57 g Carbohydrate; 7 g Fibre; 41 g Protein; 1331 mg Sodium

beef and sweet potato stew

Add more coriander and chili powder if you like their taste in this colourful stew.

Peanut (or cooking) oil	1 tbsp.	15 mL	Heat first amount of peanut oil in large saucepan or Dutch oven on medium-high. Cook beef in 2 batches, for about 5 minutes per batch, until browned. Transfer to plate. Set aside.
Beef inside round (or blade or chuck) steak, cut into 1 inch (2.5 cm) cubes	2 lbs.	900 g	
Peanut (or cooking) oil	1 tbsp.	15 mL	Heat second amount of peanut oil in same saucepan on medium. Add onion. Cook for 5 to 10 minutes, stirring often, until softened.
Large onion, chopped	1	1	
Ground coriander	2 tsp.	10 mL	Add next 3 ingredients. Heat and stir for 1 to 2 minutes until fragrant.
Garlic powder	1 tsp.	5 mL	
Chili powder	1/2 tsp.	2 mL	
Prepared beef broth	2 cups	500 mL	Add beef, broth and tomato paste. Stir. Bring to a boil. Reduce heat to low. Cook, covered, for 1 hour, stirring occasionally.
Tomato paste (see Tip, page 64)	1/4 cup	60 mL	
Cubed fresh peeled sweet potato	2 cups	500 mL	Add next 4 ingredients. Stir. Bring to a boil. Reduce heat to medium-low. Simmer, covered, for about 45 minutes, stirring occasionally, until beef and sweet potato are tender.
Raisins	2/3 cup	150 mL	
Salt	1/2 tsp.	2 mL	
Pepper	1/2 tsp.	2 mL	
Fresh spinach leaves, lightly packed	1 1/2 cups	375 mL	Add spinach and peanut butter. Heat and stir for 2 to 3 minutes until combined and spinach is wilted. Makes about 6 cups (1.5 L). Serves 6.
Smooth peanut butter	1/3 cup	75 mL	

1 serving: 531 Calories; 25.9 g Total Fat (11.5 g Mono, 4.2 g Poly, 7.8 g Sat); 83 mg Cholesterol; 37 g Carbohydrate; 5 g Fibre; 40 g Protein; 662 mg Sodium

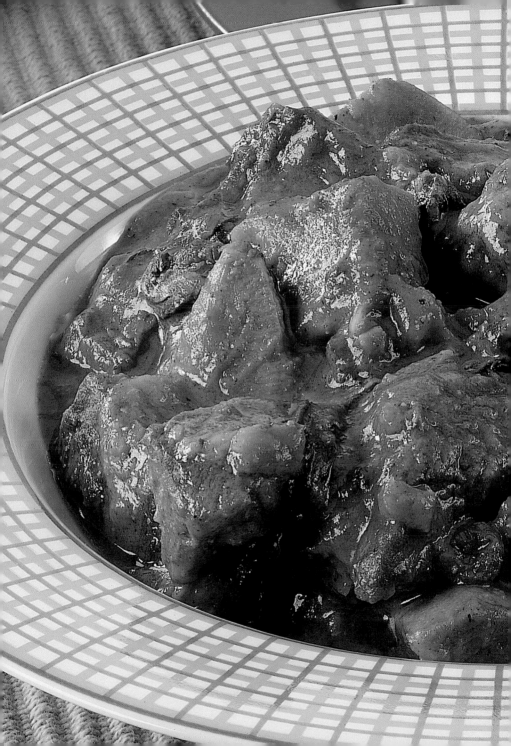

beef and eggplant stew

Taste the Mediterranean with this wonderful combination of eggplant, artichoke hearts and olives. Serve with ciabatta bread and the rest of the red wine!

Olive (or cooking) oil	2 tsp.	10 mL
Stewing beef	1 lb.	454 g
Olive (or cooking) oil	2 tsp.	10 mL
Cubed eggplant (with peel)	4 cups	1 L
Chopped onion	1 1/2 cups	375 mL
Can of diced tomatoes (with juice)	14 oz.	398 mL
Dry (or alcohol-free) red wine	3/4 cup	175 mL
Tomato paste (see Tip, page 64)	1/4 cup	60 mL
Can of artichoke hearts, drained and quartered	14 oz.	398 mL
Kalamata olives, pitted	1/4 cup	60 mL
Chopped fresh mint leaves (or 1 1/2 tsp., 7 mL, dried)	2 tbsp.	30 mL

Heat first amount of olive oil in large saucepan or Dutch oven on medium-high. Cook beef in 2 batches, for about 5 minutes per batch, stirring occasionally, until browned. Transfer to plate. Set aside.

Add second amount of olive oil to same saucepan. Reduce heat to medium. Add eggplant and onion. Cook for 5 to 10 minutes, stirring often, until onion is softened.

Add next 3 ingredients. Stir. Bring to a boil. Add beef. Stir. Reduce heat to medium-low. Simmer, covered, for about 1 1/2 hours, stirring occasionally, until beef is tender. Bring to a boil. Reduce heat to medium. Boil gently, uncovered, for about 10 minutes, stirring occasionally, until sauce is thickened.

Add remaining 3 ingredients. Stir. Cook for 3 to 5 minutes, stirring occasionally, until heated through. Makes about 6 cups (1.5 L). Serves 4.

1 serving: *382 Calories; 15.7 g Total Fat (8.1 g Mono, 1.1 g Poly, 4.8 g Sat); 63 mg Cholesterol; 26 g Carbohydrate; 7 g Fibre; 30 g Protein; 474 mg Sodium*

hungarian goulash

Travel through the Hungarian countryside and you can still see strings of bright red peppers (paprika) hanging from the rafters of farmhouses. Once the peppers dry, they're ground into the country's famous paprika powder.

All-purpose flour	1/4 cup	60 mL
Hungarian paprika	2 tsp.	10 mL
Salt	1/4 tsp.	1 mL
Pepper	1/2 tsp.	2 mL
Boneless beef round (or sirloin or blade) steak, cut into 3/4 inch (2 cm) cubes	1 1/2 lbs.	680 g
Cooking oil	2 tsp.	10 mL
Large onion, thinly sliced	1	1
Large red pepper, cut into slivers	1	1
Garlic cloves, minced (or 1/2 tsp., 2 mL, powder)	2	2
Caraway seed	1/8 tsp.	0.5 mL
Sliced carrot	2 cups	500 mL
Condensed beef broth	1 1/2 cups	375 mL
Tomato paste (see Tip, page 64)	2 tbsp.	30 mL
Hungarian paprika	2 tsp.	10 mL
Fat-free sour cream	1 cup	250 mL

Combine first 4 ingredients in large resealable freezer bag. Add beef. Seal bag. Toss until coated. Place beef in lightly greased roasting pan. Bake, uncovered, in 425°F (220°C) oven for about 10 minutes, stirring once, until browned. Transfer to bowl. Set aside.

Heat cooking oil in large saucepan or Dutch oven on medium. Add next 4 ingredients. Cook for about 5 minutes, stirring often, until onion is softened.

Add beef and next 4 ingredients. Stir. Bring to a boil. Reduce heat to medium-low. Simmer, covered, for about 1 hour until beef is tender. Remove from heat.

Stir in sour cream (see Tip, page 64). Makes about 6 cups (1.5 L). Serves 6.

1 serving: 230 Calories; 6.1 g Total Fat (4.6 g Mono, 1.8 g Poly, 1.8 g Sat); 53 mg Cholesterol; 17 g Carbohydrate; 2 g Fibre; 27 g Protein; 524 mg Sodium

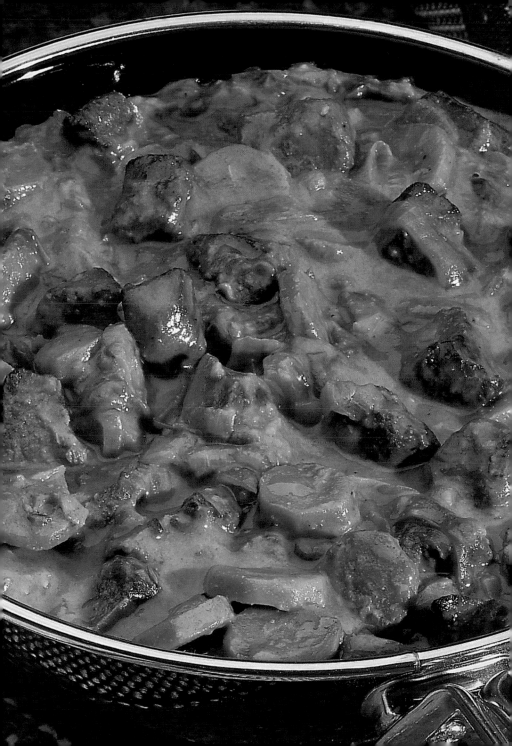

pasta and stew

Young cowpokes will love the Western look of the wagon-wheel pasta.
If you've run out, substitute any other spoon-sized pasta.

All-purpose flour	3 tbsp.	50 mL
Paprika	1 tsp.	5 mL
Salt	1 tsp.	5 mL
Pepper	1/4 tsp.	1 mL
Boneless beef round (or blade) steak, cut into 1 inch (2.5 cm) cubes	1 1/2 lbs.	680 g
Olive (or cooking) oil	2 tbsp.	30 mL
Olive (or cooking) oil	1 tsp.	5 mL
Medium onion, cut into large chunks	1	1
Chopped fresh thyme (or 3/4 tsp., 4 mL, dried)	1 tbsp.	15 mL
Garlic clove, minced	1	1
Cans of condensed beef broth (10 oz., 284 mL, each)	2	2
Can of diced tomatoes, with juice	14 oz.	398 mL
Barbecue sauce	1/4 cup	60 mL
Bay leaf	1	1
Medium carrots, sliced	4	4
Sliced fresh white mushrooms	2 cups	500 mL
Rotelle (wagon wheel) pasta, uncooked	1 1/2 cups	375 mL
Celery rib, sliced	1	1

Combine first 4 ingredients in large resealable freezer bag. Add beef. Seal bag. Toss until coated. Heat first amount of olive oil in large saucepan or Dutch oven on medium-high. Cook beef in 2 batches, for about 5 minutes per batch, stirring occasionally, until browned. Transfer to plate. Set aside.

Heat second amount of olive oil in same saucepan on medium. Add next 3 ingredients. Cook for 5 to 10 minutes, stirring often, until onion is softened.

Add beef and next 4 ingredients. Stir. Bring to a boil. Reduce heat to medium-low. Simmer, covered, for 1 1/2 hours.

Add carrot. Stir. Simmer, covered, for 30 minutes.

Add remaining 3 ingredients. Stir. Simmer, covered, for about 20 minutes until pasta is tender but firm. Discard bay leaf. Makes about 8 cups (2 L). Serves 6.

1 serving: 364 Calories; 10.7 g Total Fat (6.0 g Mono, 1.1 g Poly, 2.3 g Sat); 53 mg Cholesterol; 35 g Carbohydrate; 4 g Fibre; 32 g Protein; 1274 mg Sodium

beef bourguignon

When the French make this classic stew, a wine from Burgundy is an essential ingredient.

All-purpose flour	1/4 cup	60 mL
Salt	1/4 tsp.	1 mL
Pepper	1/4 tsp.	1 mL
Boneless beef round (or blade or sirloin) steak, cut into 3/4 inch (2 cm) cubes	2 lbs.	900 g
Dry (or alcohol-free) red wine	2 cups	500 mL
Can of condensed beef consommé	10 oz.	284 mL
Bay leaves	2	2
Cooking oil	1 1/2 tsp.	7 mL
Sliced fresh white mushrooms	2 cups	500 mL
Garlic clove, minced (or 1/4 tsp., 1 mL, powder)	1	1
Pepper, sprinkle		
Thinly sliced carrot	3 1/2 cups	875 mL
Pearl onions, peeled (see Tip, page 64)	2 cups	500 mL
Chopped fresh parsley (or 3 tsp., 15 mL, flakes)	1/4 cup	60 mL
Sprigs of fresh parsley, for garnish		

Combine first 3 ingredients in large resealable freezer bag. Add beef. Seal bag. Toss until coated. Place beef in lightly greased roasting pan. Bake, uncovered, in 425°F (220°C) oven for about 10 minutes, stirring once, until browned.

Add next 3 ingredients. Stir. Reduce heat to 350°F (175°C). Bake, covered, for 2 to 2 1/2 hours until beef is tender.

Heat cooking oil in medium frying pan on medium. Add next 3 ingredients. Cook for about 10 minutes, stirring often, until mushrooms are browned. Add to beef mixture.

Add next 3 ingredients. Stir. Bake, covered, for about 1 hour until vegetables are tender. Discard bay leaves.

Garnish with parsley. Makes about 7 1/2 cups (1.9 L). Serves 6.

1 serving: 288 Calories; 7.0 g Total Fat (3.1 g Mono, 0.7 g Poly, 2.0 g Sat); 70 mg Cholesterol; 16 g Carbohydrate; 3 g Fibre; 33 g Protein; 535 mg Sodium

stout beef stew

Ireland is home to some of the most popular stout—or strong—beers, which are dark-coloured and richly flavourful.

All-purpose flour	1/2 cup	125 mL
Seasoned salt	1 tsp.	5 mL
Pepper, sprinkle		
Stewing beef	2 lbs.	900 g
Cooking spray		
Hard margarine	1 tbsp.	15 mL
Cooking oil	1 tbsp.	15 mL
Medium onions, thinly sliced in rings	2	2
Sliced fresh white mushrooms	2 cups	500 mL
Garlic cloves, crushed (or 1/2 tsp., 2 mL, powder)	2	2
Water	2 cups	500 mL
Stout beer	1 1/3 cups	325 mL
Can of tomato paste	5 1/2 oz.	156 mL
White vinegar	1 tsp.	5 mL
Bay leaves	3	3

Salt, sprinkle

Combine first 3 ingredients in large resealable freezer bag. Add beef. Seal bag. Toss until coated. Reserve remaining flour mixture. Arrange beef in single layer on greased baking sheet with sides. Spray with cooking spray. Broil on top rack in oven for about 5 minutes, turning several times, until browned. Set aside.

Melt margarine in cooking oil in Dutch oven on medium-high. Add next 3 ingredients. Cook for about 10 minutes, stirring often, until onion is softened and mushrooms are browned.

Sprinkle with reserved flour mixture. Heat and stir for 1 minute. Slowly stir in water and beer until boiling and slightly thickened. Add next 3 ingredients. Stir. Add beef. Bake, covered, in 325°F (160°C) oven for 1 hour. Reduce heat to 300°F (150°C). Bake for about 1 1/2 hours until beef is tender. Discard bay leaves.

Sprinkle with salt. Makes about 7 cups (1.75 L). Serves 6.

1 serving: 291 Calories; 9.3 g Total Fat (4.6 g Mono, 1.3 g Poly, 2.3 g Sat); 59 mg Cholesterol; 21 g Carbohydrate; 3 g Fibre; 27 g Protein; 94 mg Sodium

green chili stew

Serve this colourful dish with orzo pasta or rice to soak up the deep brown sauce.

Baby carrots, cut into thirds	1/2 lb.	225 g
Finely chopped onion	1 cup	250 mL
Can of diced green chilies	4 oz.	113 g
Medium red pepper, diced	1	1
Garlic cloves, minced (or 1/2 tsp., 2 mL, powder)	2	2
All-purpose flour	3 tbsp.	50 mL
Chili powder	1 tbsp.	15 mL
Dried oregano	1 tsp.	5 mL
Ground cumin	1/2 tsp.	2 mL
Beef inside round (or blade or chuck) steak, trimmed of fat and cubed	2 lbs.	900 g
Cooking oil	1 tbsp.	15 mL
Water	1/2 cup	125 mL
All-purpose flour	1 tbsp.	15 mL
Dry (or alcohol -free) red wine	1/2 cup	125 mL
Beef bouillon powder	1 tsp.	5 mL
Chopped fresh parsley, for garnish		

Combine first 5 ingredients in ungreased 3 quart (3 L) casserole.

Combine next 4 ingredients in large resealable freezer bag. Add beef. Seal bag. Toss until coated. Heat cooking oil in large frying pan on medium-high. Cook beef in 2 batches, stirring occasionally, until browned. Transfer beef with slotted spoon to onion mixture.

Stir water into second amount of flour in small bowl until smooth. Stir in wine. Heat and stir on medium in same frying pan, scraping any brown bits from bottom of pan, until boiling and thickened.

Add bouillon powder. Stir until dissolved. Pour over beef mixture. Stir gently. Bake, covered, in 325°F (160°C) oven for about 2 1/2 hours until beef is tender.

Garnish with parsley. Makes about 6 cups (1.5 L).

1 cup (250 mL): 270 Calories; 6.0 g Total Fat (2.6 g Mono, 0.9 g Poly, 1.3 g Sat); 65 mg Cholesterol; 13 g Carbohydrate; 2 g Fibre; 37 g Protein; 336 mg Sodium

squash stew

Slow cooking at its finest. The low temperature and the lengthy simmer tenderize the beef and bring out the sweetness of the vegetables.

Butternut squash, peeled and cubed	2 lbs.	900 g
Diced peeled potato	3 cups	750 mL
Sliced carrot	3 cups	750 mL
Stewing beef, trimmed of fat	1 lb.	454 g
Coarsely chopped onion	1 cup	250 mL
Boiling water	1/2 cup	125 mL
Beef bouillon powder	2 tsp.	10 mL
Can of tomato sauce	7 1/2 oz.	213 mL
Granulated sugar	1/2 tsp.	2 mL
Salt	1/2 tsp.	2 mL
Pepper	1/8 tsp.	0.5 mL

Layer first 5 ingredients, in order given, in ungreased 4 quart (4 L) casserole or medium roasting pan. Set aside.

Combine boiling water and bouillon powder in medium heatproof bowl. Stir until dissolved.

Add remaining 4 ingredients. Stir. Pour over onion. Bake, covered, in 300°F (150°C) oven for 3 1/2 to 4 hours until beef and vegetables are tender. Makes about 12 cups (3 L). Serves 4.

1 serving: 454 Calories; 8.9 g Total Fat (3.2 g Mono, 0.7 g Poly, 3.1 g Sat); 56 mg Cholesterol; 65 g Carbohydrate; 9 g Fibre; 32 g Protein; 1094 mg Sodium

apricot beef

Here's an easy, kid-friendly stew that freezes well. Serve with your favourite noodles.

Stewing beef	2 lbs.	900 g
Finely chopped onion	1 1/2 cups	375 mL
Can of apricot halves with light syrup, processed in blender	14 oz.	398 mL
Brown sugar, packed	1 tsp.	5 mL
Tomato sauce	1/4 cup	60 mL
White vinegar	2 tsp.	10 mL
Worcestershire sauce	2 tsp.	10 mL
Ground allspice	1/4 tsp.	1 mL
Ground ginger	1/4 tsp.	1 mL
Salt	1 tsp.	5 mL
Pepper	1/4 tsp.	1 mL

Place beef in 3 quart (3 L) casserole. Sprinkle onion over top. Bake, uncovered, in 400°F (205°C) oven for 20 minutes, stirring at halftime.

Add remaining 9 ingredients. Stir. Reduce heat to 325°F (160°C). Bake, covered, for 2 1/2 to 3 hours until tender. Makes about 5 cups (1.25 L). Serves 8.

1 serving: 620 Calories; 15.2 g Total Fat (6.6 g Mono, 0.7 g Poly, 5.7 g Sat); 70 mg Cholesterol; 104 g Carbohydrate; 13 g Fibre; 25 g Protein; 409 mg Sodium

chickpea stew

Chickpeas are high in protein, fibre and iron. We've called for dried chickpeas here, and you don't even need to pre-soak them for this slow cooker recipe.

Water	5 1/2 cups	1.4 L
Dried chickpeas (garbanzo beans)	2 1/2 cups	625 mL
Chopped onion	1 1/2 cups	375 mL
Medium carrots, julienned (see Tip, page 64)	2	2
Dried basil	1/2 tsp.	2 mL
Pepper	1/4 tsp.	1 mL
Cooking oil	1 1/2 tsp.	7 mL
Stewing beef (or pork)	1 lb.	454 g
Can of diced tomatoes, drained and juice reserved	14 oz.	398 mL
Beef bouillon powder	1 tbsp.	15 mL
Salt	1 tsp.	5 mL
Reserved juice from tomatoes		
All-purpose flour	3 tbsp.	50 mL

Combine first 6 ingredients in 3 1/2 to 4 quart (3.5 to 4 L) slow cooker.

Heat cooking oil in large frying pan on medium-high. Add beef. Cook for about 5 minutes, stirring often, until browned. Add to slow cooker. Stir. Cook, covered, on Low for 8 to 10 hours or on High for 4 to 5 hours.

Add next 3 ingredients. Stir.

Stir reserved juice into flour in small bowl until smooth. Add to slow cooker. Stir. Cook, covered, on Low for 2 hours or on High for 1 hour. Stir before serving. Makes about 9 1/2 cups (2.3 L).

1 cup (250 mL): 300 Calories; 8.1 g Total Fat (0.7 g Mono, 0.4 g Poly, 0.5 g Sat); 7 mg Cholesterol; 37 g Carbohydrate; 1 g Fibre; 21 g Protein; 589 mg Sodium

meatball stew

Store-bought meatballs make this stew a snap to put together. Preparing it in a slow cooker makes it even easier!

Chopped onion	1 1/2 cups	375 mL
Baby carrots	3 1/2 cups	875 mL
Baby potatoes, larger ones cut in half	2 lbs.	900 g
Dried dillweed	1 1/2 tsp.	7 mL
Pepper	1/2 tsp.	2 mL
Box of frozen cooked meatballs	2 1/4 lbs.	1 kg
Can of condensed cream of mushroom soup	10 oz.	284 mL
Prepared beef broth	1 cup	250 mL
Water	1/2 cup	125 mL
Worcestershire sauce	2 tsp.	10 mL
Frozen peas	1 1/2 cups	375 mL

Layer first 3 ingredients, in order given, in 5 to 7 quart (5 to 7 L) slow cooker.

Sprinkle with dill and pepper. Arrange meatballs over top.

Combine next 4 ingredients in medium bowl. Pour over meatballs. Cook, covered, on Low for 8 to 10 hours or on High for 4 to 5 hours.

Add peas. Stir. Cook, covered, on High for 5 to 10 minutes until heated through. Makes about 15 1/2 cups (3.9 L). Serves 8.

1 serving: 506 Calories; 22.8 g Total Fat (0.1 g Mono, 0.3 g Poly, 8.8 g Sat); 56 mg Cholesterol; 45 g Carbohydrate; 5 g Fibre; 29 g Protein; 1288 mg Sodium

chicken and root vegetable stew

For a heart-healthy stew, use low-sodium or homemade chicken stock—this will also allow the delicate white-wine flavour to come through.

All-purpose flour	3 tbsp.	50 mL
Bone-in, chicken thighs, skin removed and trimmed of fat (see Tip, page 64)	2 1/2 lbs.	1.1 kg
Olive (or cooking) oil	2 tsp.	10 mL
Large carrots, chopped	2	2
Large onion, cut in half lengthwise and sliced	1	1
Large peeled potato, chopped	1	1
Small yellow turnip (or rutabaga), chopped	1	1
Chicken stock	1 cup	250 mL
Dry (or alcohol-free) white wine	1 cup	250 mL
Pepper	1/4 tsp.	1 mL
Frozen peas	1/2 cup	125 mL

Put flour into large resealable freezer bag. Add chicken. Seal bag. Toss until coated. Heat olive oil in large saucepan or Dutch oven on medium. Cook chicken in 2 batches, for about 6 minutes per batch, until browned.

Add next 7 ingredients. Stir. Bring to a boil. Reduce heat to low. Cook, covered, for 20 minutes. Simmer, uncovered, for another 30 minutes, stirring occasionally. Increase heat to medium-high. Boil for about 5 minutes until chicken is very tender and sauce is slightly thickened.

Add peas. Stir. Cook for about 3 minutes until heated through. Makes about 9 cups (2.25 L). Serves 6.

1 serving: 268 Calories; 10.1 g Total Fat (4.3 g Mono, 2.1 g Poly, 2.6 g Sat); 75 mg Cholesterol; 19 g Carbohydrate; 3 g Fibre; 24 g Protein; 107 mg Sodium

coq au vin

Traditionally, the French slowly simmered an old rooster (coq) in wine (vin) until its meat was deliciously tender. Slices of crusty bread will absorb the tasty sauce.

Hard margarine (butter browns too fast)	1/4 cup	60 mL
Boneless, skinless chicken breast halves (4 – 6 oz., 113 – 170 g, each)	8	8
Salt, sprinkle		
Pepper, sprinkle		
Pearl onions, peeled (see Tip, page 64)	12–20	12–20
Chopped onion	1/2 cup	125 mL
Fresh whole white mushrooms	1/2 lb.	225 g
Bacon slices, diced	6	6
Garlic clove, crushed (or 1/4 tsp., 1 mL, powder)	1	1
All-purpose flour	1 tbsp.	15 mL
Dry (or alcohol -free) red wine	1 cup	250 mL
Fresh parsley sprigs	2	2
Bay leaf	1	1
Dried thyme	1/4 tsp.	1 mL
Chopped parsley, for garnish		

Melt margarine in large frying pan on medium. Cook chicken in 2 batches, for 4 to 5 minutes per side until browned. Sprinkle with salt and pepper. Transfer to small roasting pan.

Add next 5 ingredients to same frying pan. Cook, stirring often, until bacon is crisp.

Sprinkle with flour. Heat and stir for 1 minute. Slowly stir in wine, scraping any brown bits from bottom of pan, until boiling and slightly thickened.

Add next 3 ingredients. Stir. Pour over chicken. Bake, covered, in 325°F (160°C) oven for about 1 hour until chicken is no longer pink inside. Discard parsley and bay leaf.

Garnish with chopped parsley. Serves 8.

1 serving: 290 Calories; 10.9 g Total Fat (5.8 g Mono, 1.5 g Poly, 2.6 g Sat); 83 mg Cholesterol; 8 g Carbohydrate; 1 g Fibre; 34 g Protein; 223 mg Sodium

cajun chicken

A slow cooker makes this such an easy treat. Serve with a hearty rye or pumpernickel bread. Leftovers freeze well.

Cooking oil	2 tbsp.	30 mL
Chopped onion	2 cups	500 mL
Chopped red pepper	1 1/2 cups	375 mL
Chopped celery	1/2 cup	125 mL
Garlic cloves, minced (or 1 tsp., 5 mL, powder)	4	4
All-purpose flour	2 tbsp.	30 mL
Sliced green onion	1/3 cup	75 mL
Lean kielbasa (or smoked ham) sausage ring, halved lengthwise and cut into 6 pieces	10 oz.	285 g
Boneless, skinless chicken thighs (about 3 oz., 85 g, each)	2 lbs.	900 g
Bay leaf	1	1
Can of condensed chicken broth	10 oz.	284 mL
Chili sauce	1/2 cup	125 mL
Chili powder	1 1/2 tsp.	7 mL
Dried basil	1/2 tsp.	2 mL
Dried oregano	1/2 tsp.	2 mL
Ground thyme	1/4 tsp.	1 mL
Pepper	1/4 tsp.	1 mL

Sprigs of fresh thyme, for garnish

Heat cooking oil in large frying pan on medium-high. Add next 4 ingredients. Cook for about 5 minutes, stirring often, until onion is softened.

Sprinkle with flour. Heat and stir for 1 minute. Transfer to 4 to 5 quart (4 to 5 L) slow cooker.

Layer next 3 ingredients, in order given, over vegetable mixture. Add bay leaf.

Combine next 7 ingredients in same frying pan. Heat and stir on medium for 5 minutes, scraping any brown bits from bottom of pan. Pour over chicken. Cook, covered, on Low for 7 to 8 hours or on High for 3 1/2 to 4 hours. Discard bay leaf.

Garnish with thyme sprigs. Makes about 6 cups (1.5 L). Serves 8.

1 serving: 275 Calories; 13.8 g Total Fat (4.7 g Mono, 2.7 g Poly, 2.3 g Sat); 63 mg Cholesterol; 13 g Carbohydrate; 1 g Fibre; 24 g Protein; 1106 mg Sodium

french bistro stew

This delicious slow-cooker dish pairs well with potatoes. Add a baguette and voilà, dinner is served.

Bacon slices, diced	2	2
Medium onion, sliced	1	1
Chopped fresh white mushrooms	1 cup	250 mL
All-purpose flour	2 tbsp.	30 mL
Diced carrot	1 1/2 cups	375 mL
Diced celery (with leaves)	1 1/2 cups	375 mL
Bone-in chicken parts, skin removed (see Tip, page 64)	3 lbs.	1.4 kg
Can of condensed chicken broth	10 oz.	284 mL
Parsley flakes	1 tbsp.	15 mL
Dried sage	1/2 tsp.	2 mL
Dried thyme	1/2 tsp.	2 mL
Salt	1/4 tsp.	1 mL
Pepper	1/4 tsp.	1 mL
Sour cream	2/3 cup	150 mL
All-purpose flour	2 tbsp.	30 mL

Cook bacon in large frying pan on medium-high until crisp. Do not drain. Add onion and mushrooms. Cook for 3 to 4 minutes, stirring often, until onion is softened.

Sprinkle with first amount of flour. Heat and stir for 1 minute. Transfer to 4 to 5 quart (4 to 5 L) slow cooker.

Layer next 3 ingredients, in order given, over mushroom mixture.

Combine next 6 ingredients in same frying pan. Heat and stir on medium for about 5 minutes, scraping any brown bits from bottom of pan, until heated through. Pour over chicken. Cook, covered, on Low for 7 to 8 hours or on High for 3 1/2 to 4 hours. Transfer chicken to serving dish using slotted spoon. Cover to keep warm.

Stir sour cream into second amount of flour in small bowl until smooth. Add to slow cooker. Stir. Cook, covered, on High for about 5 minutes until slightly thickened. Pour over chicken. Serves 6.

1 serving: 274 Calories; 11.4 g Total Fat (4.8 g Mono, 1.8 g Poly, 5.4 g Sat); 95 mg Cholesterol; 13 g Carbohydrate; 2 g Fibre; 29 g Protein; 600 mg Sodium

lamb stew with winter vegetables

Simmered to perfection with classic winter vegetables, this is a splendid dish to enjoy after a day outdoors. Add dumplings for an extra treat. This recipe is easily doubled—just use a larger Dutch oven.

All-purpose flour	1/4 cup	60 mL
Salt	1/2 tsp.	2 mL
Pepper	1/2 tsp.	2 mL
Lamb shoulder, trimmed of fat and cut into 1 1/2 inch (3.8 cm) cubes	1 1/2 lbs.	680 g
Cooking oil	1 tbsp.	15 mL
Cooking oil	1 tbsp.	15 mL
Large onions, chopped	2	2
Prepared beef broth	4 cups	1 L
Small yellow turnip (or rutabaga), chopped	1	1
Large carrots, chopped	2	2
Large parsnips, chopped	2	2
Large peeled potato, chopped	1	1
Dried oregano	1/2 tsp.	2 mL
Dried rosemary, crushed	1/2 tsp.	2 mL
Frozen peas	1 cup	250 mL

Combine first 3 ingredients in large resealable freezer bag. Add lamb. Seal bag. Toss until coated. Reserve remaining flour mixture. Heat first amount of cooking oil in large saucepan or Dutch oven on medium-high. Cook lamb in 2 batches, for about 5 minutes per batch, until browned. Transfer to plate. Set aside.

Heat second amount of cooking oil in same saucepan on medium-high. Add onion. Cook for about 5 minutes, stirring often, until softened. Add reserved flour mixture. Heat and stir for 1 minute.

Add broth. Heat and stir for 2 to 3 minutes until boiling and slightly thickened. Add lamb and next 6 ingredients. Stir. Bring to a boil. Reduce heat to medium-low. Simmer, covered, for about 1 1/2 hours, stirring occasionally, until lamb is tender.

Add peas. Stir. Cook for about 5 minutes until heated through. Makes about 7 cups (1.75 L). Serves 4.

1 serving: 687 Calories; 26.2 g Total Fat (10.8 g Mono, 3.7 g Poly, 8.9 g Sat); 129 mg Cholesterol; 66 g Carbohydrate; 8 g Fibre; 46 g Protein; 1848 mg Sodium

minted lamb and pea braise

Boiled baby potatoes or a slice of hearty bread would make a fast side for this succulent stew.

All-purpose flour	2 tbsp.	30 mL
Stewing lamb	1 lb.	454 g
Cooking oil	1 tbsp.	15 mL
Cooking oil	1 tsp.	5 mL
Small onions, quartered	2	2
Small carrots, cut into 3/4 inch (2 cm) pieces	4	4
Spiced apple cider	1 cup	250 mL
Frozen peas	1 cup	250 mL
Chopped fresh mint	1/4 cup	60 mL

Put flour into large resealable freezer bag. Add lamb. Seal bag. Toss until coated. Heat first amount of cooking oil in large saucepan on medium-high. Cook lamb in 2 batches, for 5 to 6 minutes per batch, stirring occasionally, until browned. Transfer to plate. Set aside.

Heat second amount of cooking oil in same saucepan on medium. Add onion. Cook for 5 to 10 minutes, stirring often, until softened.

Add lamb, carrot and cider. Stir. Bring to a boil. Reduce heat to medium-low. Simmer, covered, for about 1 1/2 hours, stirring occasionally, until lamb is tender. Bring to a boil on medium. Boil gently, uncovered, for about 5 minutes, stirring occasionally, until sauce is thickened. Reduce heat to medium-low.

Add peas and mint. Stir. Cook for about 5 minutes until heated through. Makes about 3 1/2 cups (875 mL). Serves 4.

1 serving: 408 Calories; 24.4 g Total Fat (10.7 g Mono, 3.1 g Poly, 8.8 g Sat); 78 mg Cholesterol; 23 g Carbohydrate; 4 g Fibre; 24 g Protein; 130 mg Sodium

special curry

To save time, prepare the vegetables right after you've set the meat to cook. And if you like life well-spiced, add extra curry powder. This is wonderful over rice.

Stewing lamb (or beef)	2 lbs.	900 g
Water	3 cups	750 mL
Chopped onion	1 1/2 cups	375 mL
Beef bouillon powder	1 tbsp.	15 mL
Large peeled cooking apples (such as McIntosh), cubed	2	2
Medium carrots, diced	2	2
Crushed pineapple, with juice	1 cup	250 mL
Chopped celery	1/2 cup	125 mL
Raisins	1/3 cup	75 mL
Mango chutney	2 tbsp.	30 mL
Plum jam	2 tbsp.	30 mL
Granulated sugar	4 tsp.	20 mL
Curry powder	2 tsp.	10 mL
Salt	2 tsp.	10 mL
Pepper	1 tsp.	5 mL
Water	1/4 cup	60 mL
Cornstarch	1/4 cup	60 mL

Combine first 4 ingredients in large saucepan. Bring to a boil. Reduce heat to medium-low. Simmer, covered, for 1 hour.

Add next 11 ingredients. Stir. Bring to a boil. Reduce heat to medium-low. Simmer, covered, for about 30 minutes until lamb is tender.

Stir water into cornstarch in small cup. Add to lamb mixture. Heat and stir until boiling and thickened. Makes about 9 cups (2.25 L). Serves 6.

1 serving: 375 Calories; 8.5 g Total Fat (3.3 g Mono, 0.9 g Poly, 3.0 g Sat); 98 mg Cholesterol; 43 g Carbohydrate; 3 g Fibre; 32 g Protein; 1322 mg Sodium

curried pork stew

Curry powder manufacturers all have their own blend of different spices. Adventurous cooks may want to visit a South Asian grocery store to experiment with various combinations.

Cooking oil	1 tbsp.	15 mL
Stewing pork	1 lb.	454 g
Curry powder	1 1/2 tbsp.	25 mL
Chopped carrot	2 cups	500 mL
Chopped onion	1 1/2 cups	375 mL
Low-sodium prepared chicken broth	1 1/2 cups	375 mL
Chopped yellow turnip (or rutabaga)	1 cup	250 mL
Chopped celery	1/2 cup	125 mL
Tomato paste (see Tip, page 64)	1/4 cup	60 mL
Bay leaves	2	2
Pepper	1/4 tsp.	1 mL

Heat cooking oil in large saucepan or Dutch oven on medium. Add pork. Cook for about 10 minutes, stirring occasionally, until browned.

Add curry powder. Heat and stir for about 1 minute until fragrant.

Add remaining 8 ingredients. Stir. Bring to a boil. Reduce heat to medium-low. Simmer, covered, for about 1 hour, stirring occasionally, until pork is tender. Bring to a boil on medium. Boil gently, uncovered, for about 10 minutes until sauce is thickened. Discard bay leaves. Makes about 5 cups (1.25 L). Serves 4.

1 serving: 400 Calories; 24.7 g Total Fat (11.2 g Mono, 3.4 g Poly, 7.4 g Sat); 81 mg Cholesterol; 22 g Carbohydrate; 5 g Fibre; 24 g Protein; 419 mg Sodium

creamed pork and cabbage stew

Serve this with mashed potatoes for comfort food at its best.

Cooking oil	1 tbsp.	15 mL
Boneless pork loin, cut into thin strips	1 lb.	454 g
Large onion, cut in half lengthwise and sliced	1	1
Water	2 1/2 cups	625 mL
Apple juice	1/2 cup	125 mL
Beef bouillon powder	1 tbsp.	15 mL
Dry mustard	1/4 tsp.	1 mL
Ground nutmeg	1/4 tsp.	1 mL
Chopped cabbage	4 cups	1 L
Medium carrots, cut into 1/4 inch (6 mm) slices	4	4
Celery rib, sliced	1	1
Whipping cream	1 cup	250 mL
All-purpose flour	1/4 cup	60 mL

Heat cooking oil in large saucepan or Dutch oven on medium-high. Add pork. Cook for about 5 minutes, stirring occasionally, until browned.

Add onion. Cook for 3 to 4 minutes, stirring often, until onion starts to soften.

Add next 5 ingredients. Stir. Bring to a boil. Reduce heat to medium-low. Simmer, covered, for about 40 minutes, stirring occasionally, until pork is tender.

Add next 3 ingredients. Stir. Cook, covered, for about 15 minutes until vegetables are tender-crisp.

Stir whipping cream into flour in small bowl until smooth. Add to pork mixture. Heat and stir until boiling and thickened. Makes about 8 cups (2 L).

1 cup (250 mL): 252 Calories; 15.3 g Total Fat (5.4 g Mono, 1.3 g Poly, 7.6 g Sat); 68 mg Cholesterol; 14 g Carbohydrate; 2 g Fibre; 15 g Protein; 286 mg Sodium

gypsy stew

Rinsing the sauerkraut eliminates much of the sourness and makes this bacon-flavoured dish perfect with buttered noodles or mashed potatoes.

Bacon slices, diced	6	6	
Stewing pork, trimmed of fat	2 1/4 lbs.	1 kg	
Large onions, cut in half lengthwise and thinly sliced	2	2	
Paprika	4 tsp.	20 mL	
Garlic cloves, minced (or 3/4 tsp., 4 mL, powder)	3	3	
Caraway seed	1 tsp.	5 mL	
Water	2 cups	500 mL	
Jar of wine sauerkraut, rinsed and drained	17 1/2 oz.	500 mL	
Chicken bouillon powder	1 tsp.	5 mL	
Sour cream	1 cup	250 mL	
All-purpose flour	2 tbsp.	30 mL	
Salt, sprinkle			
Pepper, sprinkle			
Bacon slice, cooked crisp and crumbled	1	1	

Cook first amount of bacon in large saucepan or Dutch oven on medium until almost crisp. Drain all but 1 tbsp. (15 mL) drippings.

Add next 5 ingredients. Cook for about 10 minutes, stirring often, until onion is softened and bacon is crisp.

Stir in water. Bring to a boil. Reduce heat to medium-low. Simmer, covered, for 1 hour.

Add sauerkraut and bouillon powder. Stir. Bring to a boil. Reduce heat to medium-low. Simmer, covered, for 45 to 60 minutes until pork is tender.

Stir sour cream into flour in small bowl until smooth. Add to pork mixture. Heat and stir on low for about 10 minutes until boiling and slightly thickened. Stir in salt and pepper.

Sprinkle second amount of bacon over individual servings. Makes about 8 cups (2 L).

1 cup (250 mL): 410 Calories; 28.2 g Total Fat (11.8 g Mono, 2.8 g Poly, 11.2 g Sat); 95 mg Cholesterol; 10 g Carbohydrate; 2 g Fibre; 28 g Protein; 728 mg Sodium

pork cassoulet

Dried navy beans are another option for this tasty classic.

Dried Great Northern beans	2 cups	500 mL
Lean pork sausages	1 3/4 lbs.	790 g
Olive (or cooking) oil	1 tbsp.	15 mL
Pork shoulder picnic roast, cut into 1 inch (2.5 cm) cubes	3 lbs.	1.4 kg
Olive (or cooking) oil	1 tbsp.	15 mL
Medium onions, sliced	2	2
Garlic cloves, minced	4	4
Bacon slices, diced	4	4
Prepared chicken broth	2 cups	500 mL
Dry red wine	3/4 cup	175 mL
Can of tomato paste	5 1/2 oz.	156 mL
Chopped fresh thyme	1 1/2 tbsp.	25 mL
Salt	2 tsp.	10 mL
Pepper	1/2 tsp.	2 mL
Fine dry bread crumbs	3/4 cup	175 mL

Place beans in large heatproof bowl. Add boiling water to cover. Let stand for 2 hours until doubled in size. Drain. Transfer beans to large saucepan. Add water until 2 inches (5 cm) above beans. Bring to a boil.

Reduce heat to low. Cook, partially covered, for about 1 hour until tender but firm. Drain. Set aside.

Cook sausages in large frying pan on medium for about 15 minutes, turning occasionally, until no longer pink inside. Transfer to cutting board. Cut into 2 inch (5 cm) pieces. Set aside. Drain drippings.

Heat first amount of olive oil in same frying pan on medium-high. Cook pork in 2 batches, stirring occasionally, until browned. Transfer to plate. Set aside.

Heat second amount of olive oil in same frying pan on medium-high. Add onion and garlic. Cook for about 5 minutes, stirring often, until onion is softened. Add bacon. Cook for about 10 minutes until bacon is crisp.

Combine beans, sausages, pork and onion mixture in large roasting pan or Dutch oven. Combine next 6 ingredients in medium bowl. Pour over pork mixture. Bake, covered, in 350°F (175°C) oven for about 1 1/2 hours until pork is tender.

Sprinkle with bread crumbs. Bake, uncovered, for about 20 minutes until top is crisp. Broil for about 5 minutes until golden. Makes about 13 cups (3.25 L). Serves 8.

1 serving: 828 Calories; 44 g Total Fat (17.4 g Mono, 12.3 g Poly, 15.3 g Sat); 109 mg Cholesterol; 60 g Carbohydrate; 8 g Fibre; 45 g Protein; 1675 mg Sodium

cioppino

A fish stew created by Italian immigrants in San Fransisco, cioppino (chup-PEE-noh) is often served with Italian bread to soak up every last bit of flavour.

Hard margarine (or butter)	1 tbsp.	15 mL
Olive (or cooking) oil	2 tbsp.	30 mL
Thinly sliced leeks (white part only)	2 cups	500 mL
Chopped green pepper	1/2 cup	125 mL
Garlic cloves, minced (or 3/4 tsp., 4 mL, powder)	3	3
Small whole fresh white mushrooms	3 cups	750 mL
Can of stewed tomatoes (with juice), mashed	14 oz.	398 mL
Dry (or alcohol-free) red wine	1 1/2 cups	375 mL
Can of tomato paste	5 1/2 oz.	156 mL
Lemon juice	3 tbsp.	50 mL
Dried basil	2 tsp.	10 mL
Bay leaf	1	1
Dried oregano	1/2 tsp.	2 mL
King (or Snow) crab legs, not shelled, broken into pieces (or 9 oz., 255 g, imitation crab chunks)	1 lb.	454 g
Small bay scallops	10 oz.	285 g
Raw lobster tail, shelled and cut into 1 inch (2.5 cm) pieces	1/2 lb.	225 g
Uncooked shrimp (peeled and deveined)	1/2 lb.	225 g
Salt	1/2 tsp.	2 mL
Pepper, sprinkle		

Melt margarine in olive oil in large saucepan or Dutch oven on medium. Add next 3 ingredients. Cook for about 10 minutes, stirring often, until leek is softened.

Add next 8 ingredients. Stir. Bring to a boil. Reduce heat to medium-low. Simmer, covered, for 1 hour. Discard bay leaf.

Add remaining 6 ingredients. Stir. Cook, covered, for 8 to 10 minutes until shrimp turn pink and lobster and scallops are opaque. Makes about 10 cups (2.5 L).

1 cup (250 mL): 198 Calories; 5.2 g Total Fat (3.0 g Mono, 0.8 g Poly, 0.8 g Sat); 72 mg Cholesterol; 14 g Carbohydrate; 2 g Fibre; 19 g Protein; 553 mg Sodium

mushroom ragoût

Brown (cremini) mushrooms add a full-bodied, earthy flavour to this dish that goes well with pasta. Feel free to add an extra dash of spices. If you'd like a thicker sauce, remove the lid for the last 15 to 20 minutes.

Ingredient	Amount	Metric
Dried shiitake mushrooms	1 oz.	28 g
Boiling water	1 1/2 cups	375 mL
Olive (or cooking) oil	2 tsp.	10 mL
Diced onion	1 cup	250 mL
Garlic cloves, minced (or 1/4 – 3/4 tsp., 1 – 4 mL, powder)	1 – 3	1 – 3
Sliced fresh brown (or white) mushrooms	3 cups	750 mL
Dry (or alcohol-free) white wine	1/2 cup	125 mL
Can of stewed tomatoes (with juice), mashed	19 oz.	540 mL
Can of tomato paste	5 1/2 oz.	156 mL
Granulated sugar	1 tbsp.	15 mL
Dried basil	1 tsp.	5 mL
Bay leaf	1	1
Dried marjoram	1/2 tsp.	2 mL
Pepper	1/2 tsp.	2 mL
Dried rosemary, crushed	1/4 tsp.	1 mL
Light sour cream	6 tbsp.	100 mL
Sprigs of fresh rosemary, for garnish		

Put shiitake mushrooms into small heatproof bowl. Add boiling water. Stir. Let stand for about 20 minutes until softened. Drain, reserving liquid. Remove and discard stems. Chop. Set aside.

Heat olive oil in large frying pan on medium. Add onion and garlic. Cook for about 2 minutes, stirring often, until onion is softened. Add brown mushrooms. Cook for about 8 minutes, stirring occasionally, until liquid has evaporated and mushrooms are starting to brown. Add wine. Heat and stir until boiling.

Add next 8 ingredients, shiitake mushrooms and reserved liquid. Stir well. Bring to a boil. Reduce heat to medium-low. Simmer, covered, for 1 hour, stirring occasionally. Remove from heat. Discard bay leaf.

Stir in sour cream (see Tip, page 64).

Garnish with rosemary sprigs. Makes about 4 cups (1 L). Serves 4.

1 serving: 205 Calories; 4.9 g Total Fat (1.5 g Mono, 1.0 g Poly, 1.6 g Sat); 8 mg Cholesterol; 38 g Carbohydrate; 6 g Fibre; 8 g Protein; 176 mg Sodium

moroccan stew

Use vegetable bouillon powder if you want to create a vegetarian dish. The couscous also pairs fabulously with barbecued sausages or pork chops.

Olive (or cooking) oil	2 tbsp.	30 mL
Cubed peeled potato	2 cups	500 mL
Sliced zucchini (with peel)	2 cups	500 mL
Diced onion	1 1/2 cups	375 mL
Sliced carrot	1 1/2 cups	375 mL
Chopped green pepper	1 cup	250 mL
Water	3 cups	750 mL
Can of chickpeas (garbanzo beans), rinsed and drained	19 oz.	540 mL
Jar of roasted red peppers, drained and slivered	13 oz.	370 mL
Raisins	1/4 cup	60 mL
Sun-dried tomatoes, chopped	1/4 cup	60 mL
Chicken bouillon powder	1 tbsp.	15 mL
Ground cinnamon	1/2 tsp.	2 mL
Ground ginger	1/2 tsp.	2 mL
Turmeric	1/2 tsp.	2 mL
Cayenne pepper	1/4 tsp.	1 mL
Salt	1/4 tsp.	1 mL
Pepper	1/8 tsp.	0.5 mL
Water	1/3 cup	75 mL
Cornstarch	1 1/2 tbsp.	25 mL

CINNAMON COUSCOUS

Water	2 cups	500 mL
Chicken bouillon powder	1 tbsp.	15 mL
Hard margarine (or butter)	1 tbsp.	15 mL
Ground cinnamon	1/2 tsp.	2 mL
Plain couscous	1 1/2 cups	375 mL

Heat olive oil in large saucepan or Dutch oven on medium-high. Add next 5 ingredients. Cook for about 15 minutes, stirring often, until vegetables are tender-crisp.

Add next 12 ingredients. Stir. Bring to a boil. Reduce heat to medium-low. Simmer, covered, for about 25 minutes until vegetables are tender.

Stir second amount of water into cornstarch in small cup. Add to vegetable mixture. Heat and stir until boiling and thickened. Makes about 8 cups (2 L).

Cinnamon Couscous: Combine first 4 ingredients in large saucepan. Bring to a boil. Remove from heat. Add couscous. Stir. Let stand, covered, for 10 minutes. Fluff with fork before serving. Makes about 5 cups (1.25 L) couscous. Serve with stew.

1 cup (250 mL) stew with 6 tbsp. (90 mL) couscous: 203 Calories; 4.1 g Total Fat (2.4 g Mono, 0.7 g Poly, 0.6 g Sat); trace Cholesterol; 36 g Carbohydrate; 3 g Fibre; 6 g Protein; 625 mg Sodium

recipe index

topical tips

Adding cream to hot dishes: To prevent curdling when adding cream products to soups and stews, don't let the cream come to a boil. Bring your pot just to the boil after adding, or for extra assurance, add it after removing from the heat. When reheating cream-based dishes, heat slowly and watch closely or it may separate and curdle.

Cutting julienne: To julienne, cut into thin strips that resemble matchsticks.

Peeling pearl onions: To easily peel pearl onions, place them in a bowl and pour over boiling water to cover. Drain, cut the ends off and just slip the peels off.

Removing skin from chicken: When removing skin from chicken parts, grasp skin with a paper towel. This will give a good grip on the otherwise slippery skin.

Tomato paste leftovers: If a recipe calls for less than an entire can of tomato paste, freeze the unopened can for 30 minutes. Open both ends and push the contents through one end. Slice off only what you need. Freeze the remaining paste in a resealable freezer bag or plastic wrap for future use.

Nutrition Information Guidelines

Each recipe is analyzed using the Canadian Nutrient File from Health Canada, which is based on the United States Department of Agriculture (USDA) Nutrient Database.

- If more than one ingredient is listed (such as "butter or hard margarine"), or if a range is given (1 – 2 tsp., 5 – 10 mL), only the first ingredient or first amount is analyzed.

- For meat, poultry and fish, the serving size per person is based on the recommended 4 oz. (113 g) uncooked weight (without bone), which is 2 – 3 oz. (57 – 85 g) cooked weight (without bone) — approximately the size of a deck of playing cards.

- Milk used is 1% M.F. (milk fat), unless otherwise stated.

- Cooking oil used is canola oil, unless otherwise stated.

- Ingredients indicating "sprinkle," "optional" or "for garnish" are not included in the nutrition information.

- The fat in recipes and combination foods can vary greatly depending on the sources and types of fats used in each specific ingredient. For these reasons, the count of saturated, monounsaturated and polyunsaturated fats may not add up to the total fat content.

warm
desserts

Choice recipes from
Company's Coming cookbooks

Jean Paré

sweet almond and cardamom couscous dessert

Just as rice can be used in sweet dishes, so too can couscous. Fresh fruit, such as sliced pears, is a nice accompaniment to this dessert.

Can of evaporated milk	13 1/2 oz.	385 mL
Sweetened condensed milk	1/4 cup	60 mL
Whole green cardamom, bruised (see Tip, page 64)	6	6
Brown sugar, packed	3 tbsp.	50 mL
Ground ginger	1/4 tsp.	1 mL
Salt	1/4 tsp.	1 mL
Plain couscous	1 3/4 cups	425 mL
Slivered almonds, toasted (see Tip, page 64)	3/4 cup	175 mL

Combine first 3 ingredients in large saucepan. Bring to a boil. Remove from heat. Let stand, covered, for 10 minutes. Discard cardamom.

Add next 3 ingredients. Heat and stir on medium-low until brown sugar is dissolved. Bring to a boil. Add couscous. Stir. Remove from heat. Let stand, covered, for about 5 minutes until liquid is absorbed. Fluff with fork.

Add almonds. Stir. Serve immediately. Serves 6.

1 serving: 458 Calories; 14.2 g Total Fat (6.8 g Mono, 1.9 g Poly, 4.7 g Sat); 25 mg Cholesterol; 68 g Carbohydrate; 4 g Fibre; 16 g Protein; 198 mg Sodium

bread puddings

With sweet apples and a kiss of cinnamon, these individual puddings are on the table in less than 30 minutes. Whole-grain bread bumps up the fibre content, but white bread will do as well.

Apple juice	1/4 cup	60 mL
Chopped dried apple	1/2 cup	125 mL
Large eggs, fork-beaten	2	2
Can of skim evaporated milk	13 1/2 oz.	385 mL
Brown sugar, packed	3 tbsp.	50 mL
Vanilla extract	1 tsp.	5 mL
Ground cinnamon	1/2 tsp.	2 mL
Ground nutmeg, sprinkle		
Salt, just a pinch		
Whole-grain bread slices, cubed	4	4
Brown sugar, packed	4 tsp.	20 mL

Pour apple juice into small saucepan. Bring to a boil. Pour over dried apple in small heatproof bowl. Let stand for 10 minutes until softened.

Combine next 7 ingredients in medium bowl. Add bread cubes and dried apple mixture. Stir. Spoon into 4 greased 1 cup (250 mL) ramekins.

Sprinkle with second amount of brown sugar. Place ramekins on baking sheet with sides. Bake in 375°F (190°C) oven for about 20 minutes until top is golden and knife inserted in centre comes out clean. Let stand for 3 to 4 minutes until set. Serve warm. Serves 4.

1 serving: 327 Calories; 3.5 g Total Fat (1.5 g Mono, 0.6 g Poly, 1.0 g Sat); 93 mg Cholesterol; 61 g Carbohydrate; 3 g Fibre; 13 g Protein; 433 mg Sodium

apricot and marmalade pudding

Perfect as an after-dinner treat with ice cream, this bread pudding can also star as a Sunday brunch dish.

Boiling water		
Dried apricots, finely chopped	1/3 cup	75 mL
Baguette bread loaf, cut into 1/3 inch (1 cm) slices	1/2	1/2
Orange marmalade	1/3 cup	75 mL
Large eggs	4	4
Milk	4 cups	1 L
Granulated sugar	2/3 cup	150 mL

Pour boiling water over apricot in small heatproof bowl. Let stand for 10 minutes until softened. Drain well. Gently squeeze apricot to remove excess water.

Spread one side of each baguette slice with marmalade. Arrange, marmalade-side up and slightly overlapping, in greased shallow 2 quart (2 L) baking dish. Sprinkle with apricot.

Whisk remaining 3 ingredients in large bowl or 8 cup (2 L) liquid measure. Carefully pour half over baguette slices. Let stand for 10 minutes. Stir remaining milk mixture. Carefully pour over baguette slices. Place dish in larger baking pan. Pour boiling water into pan until halfway up sides of dish. Bake in 325°F (160°C) oven for 1 1/2 to 1 3/4 hours until set and knife inserted in centre comes out clean. Remove dish from pan. Let stand for 20 minutes before serving. Serve warm. Serves 6.

1 serving: 328 Calories; 5.8 g Total Fat (2.1 g Mono, 0.7 g Poly, 2.3 g Sat); 154 mg Cholesterol; 58 g Carbohydrate; 2 g Fibre; 12 g Protein; 255 mg Sodium

fall fruit pudding

The secret ingredient for this moist, aromatic dessert? Beets! Wear rubber gloves to grate them. Serve with lashings of custard sauce or lightly whipped and sweetened whipping cream.

Chopped pecans	3/4 cup	175 mL
Chopped red glazed cherries	3/4 cup	175 mL
Diced dried apricot	3/4 cup	175 mL
All-purpose flour	1/2 cup	125 mL
Hard margarine (or butter), softened	3/4 cup	175 mL
Brown sugar, packed	1 cup	250 mL
Vanilla extract	1 1/2 tsp.	7 mL
Large eggs	3	3
All-purpose flour	1 1/2 cups	375 mL
Baking powder	1 1/2 tsp.	7 mL
Ground cinnamon	1/2 tsp.	2 mL
Salt	1/2 tsp.	2 mL
Ground allspice	1/4 tsp.	1 mL
Ground nutmeg	1/4 tsp.	1 mL
Grated carrot	1 cup	250 mL
Frozen concentrated orange juice, thawed	1/2 cup	125 mL
Finely grated fresh beets	1 cup	250 mL
Water	1/4 cup	60 mL

Combine first 4 ingredients in medium bowl. Toss until coated. Set aside.

Cream margarine and brown sugar in large bowl. Add vanilla. Add eggs, 1 at a time, beating well after each addition.

Combine next 6 ingredients in small bowl. Add 1/3 of flour mixture to margarine mixture. Mix until no dry flour remains.

Add carrot and concentrated orange juice. Add another 1/3 of flour mixture. Mix until no dry flour remains. Add beets and water. Stir. Add remaining 1/3 of flour mixture. Stir. Add cherry mixture. Stir until no dry flour remains and fruit is coated. Spoon into greased 10 x 4 1/2 inch (25 x 11 cm) tube pan. Smooth top. Bake on bottom rack in 325°F (160°C) oven for about 1 1/4 hours until wooden pick inserted in centre comes out clean. Let stand in pan on wire rack for 20 minutes. Serve warm. Serves 12.

1 serving: 414 Calories; 19.0 g Total Fat (11.7 g Mono, 2.8 g Poly, 3.4 g Sat); 54 mg Cholesterol; 58 g Carbohydrate; 2 g Fibre; 5 g Protein; 321 mg Sodium

molten chocolate cakes

Once you've flipped the cakes onto the plate, you can keep them covered with the ramekins for up to 20 minutes, ensuring that they stay warm and the centre remains molten. A scoop or two of ice cream contrasts wonderfully with this warm dessert.

Cocoa, sifted if lumpy	1 tbsp.	15 mL
Butter (not margarine)	2/3 cup	150 mL
Semi-sweet chocolate baking squares (1 oz., 28 g, each), chopped	5	5
Egg yolks (large)	2	2
Large eggs	2	2
Icing (confectioner's) sugar	1 1/2 cups	375 mL
All-purpose flour	1/2 cup	125 mL

Sprinkle first amount of cocoa into greased 3/4 cup (175 mL) ramekin. Tilt ramekin to coat bottom and side with cocoa. Gently tap excess cocoa into another greased ramekin. Repeat 5 times for a total of 6 cocoa-dusted ramekins. Place ramekins on baking sheet with sides. Set aside.

Heat butter and chocolate in small heavy saucepan on lowest heat, stirring often, until almost melted. Do not overheat. Remove from heat. Stir until smooth. Cool slightly.

Beat egg yolks and whole eggs in medium bowl for about 2 minutes until frothy. Beat in icing sugar on low. Add chocolate mixture and flour. Beat well until thick and glossy. Spoon batter into prepared ramekins. Bake in 450°F (230°C) oven for about 12 minutes until batter rises evenly, edges appear set and middle is almost set. Let stand for 3 to 5 minutes. Run knife around sides of cakes to loosen. Cover with individual plates and invert to remove from ramekins. Serve warm. Makes 6 cakes.

1 cake: 525 Calories; 33.6 g Total Fat (10.3 g Mono, 1.6 g Poly, 19.6 g Sat); 206 mg Cholesterol; 55 g Carbohydrate; 2 g Fibre; 6 g Protein; 261 mg Sodium

sauced lemon pudding cake

Pure lemon extract takes its flavour from the oils in the lemon peel, creating a powerful citrus flavour. If you substitute juice for the extract, the flavour won't be nearly as "zesty"!

All-purpose flour	1 cup	250 mL
Granulated sugar	2/3 cup	150 mL
Juice of 1 medium lemon (see Tip, page 64), plus milk to measure	1/2 cup	125 mL
Hard margarine (or butter), softened	2 tbsp.	30 mL
Grated lemon zest	1 tbsp.	15 mL
Baking powder	2 tsp.	10 mL
Baking soda	1/4 tsp.	1 mL
Salt	1/8 tsp.	0.5 mL
Boiling water	1 3/4 cups	425 mL
Granulated sugar	1 cup	250 mL
Hard margarine (or butter)	1 tbsp.	15 mL
Lemon extract	2 tsp.	10 mL

Lemon zest, for garnish
Sprigs of fresh mint, for garnish

Measure first 8 ingredients into medium bowl. Stir until just moistened. Transfer to greased 1 1/2 quart (1.5 L) casserole.

Combine next 4 ingredients in small bowl. Stir until sugar is dissolved. Pour over flour mixture. Do not stir. Bake, uncovered, in 400°F (205°C) oven for about 30 minutes until golden and firm. Let stand for 15 minutes.

Garnish with lemon zest and mint. Serve warm. Serves 4.

1 serving: 549 Calories; 9.0 g Total Fat (5.7 g Mono, 1.0 g Poly, 1.8 g Sat); 0 mg Cholesterol; 117 g Carbohydrate; 1 g Fibre; 4 g Protein; 369 mg Sodium

sticky ginger fig cake

Figs are so tempting—many believe Adam ate a fig, instead of an apple, before creating his fig-leaf outfit. See if anyone can resist this dessert!

Water	1 1/3 cups	325 mL
Chopped dried fig	1 1/3 cups	325 mL
Baking soda	1 tsp.	5 mL
Butter (or hard margarine), softened	1/3 cup	75 mL
Brown sugar, packed	2/3 cup	150 mL
Large eggs	2	2
All-purpose flour	1 cup	250 mL
Minced crystallized ginger	1/4 cup	60 mL
Baking powder	2 tsp.	10 mL

CINNAMON BRANDY SAUCE

Brown sugar, packed	1/2 cup	125 mL
Butter (or hard margarine), cut up	1/2 cup	125 mL
Whipping cream	1/2 cup	125 mL
Brandy	2 tbsp.	30 mL
Ground cinnamon	1/2 tsp.	2 mL

Line bottom of greased deep round 8 inch (20 cm) cake (or springform) pan with parchment (not waxed) paper. Line side, extending about 2 inches (5 cm) higher than side of pan. Set aside. Bring water to a boil in medium saucepan. Add figs. Remove from heat. Add baking soda. Stir. Let stand for 10 minutes. Process in blender or food processor until almost smooth (see Safety Tip).

Cream butter and brown sugar in large bowl until brown sugar is dissolved. Add eggs, 1 at a time, beating well after each addition.

Combine next 3 ingredients in medium bowl. Add to butter mixture. Stir well. Add fig mixture. Stir well. Spread in prepared pan. Bake in 350°F (175°C) oven for about 50 minutes until wooden pick inserted in centre comes out clean. Let stand in pan for 10 minutes. Remove from pan and place on wire rack to cool. Cuts into 8 wedges.

Cinnamon Brandy Sauce: Combine all 5 ingredients in medium saucepan. Heat and stir on medium until brown sugar is dissolved and butter is melted. Bring to a boil. Reduce heat to medium. Boil gently for about 5 minutes, without stirring, until slightly thickened. Let stand 10 minutes. Makes about 1 cup (250 mL) sauce. Drizzle over warm cake. Serves 8.

1 serving: 540 Calories; 27.1 g Total Fat (7.9 g Mono, 1.3 g Poly, 16.3 g Sat); 127 mg Cholesterol; 72 g Carbohydrate; 4 g Fibre; 5 g Protein; 500 mg Sodium

Safety Tip: Follow blender manufacturer's instructions for processing hot liquids. If in doubt, we recommend using a hand blender.

cherry pear clafoutis

Classic French clafoutis (kla-FOO-tee) is a cross between a cake and a pudding. Add a dusting of icing sugar just before serving with ice cream or whipped cream.

Cans of pitted Bing cherries in heavy syrup, drained (14 oz., 398 mL, each)	3	3
Medium firm peeled pears, chopped	3	3
Large eggs	8	8
Granulated sugar	1 cup	250 mL
Vanilla extract	2 tsp.	10 mL
All-purpose flour	1 1/3 cups	325 mL
Milk	1 cup	250 mL
Whipping cream	1 cup	250 mL
Baking powder	1 1/2 tsp.	7 mL

Combine cherries and pear in greased 9 x 13 inch (22 x 33 cm) baking dish.

Beat next 3 ingredients in large bowl until thick and pale.

Add remaining 4 ingredients. Stir. Pour over fruit mixture. Bake in 375°F (190°C) oven for about 50 minutes until lightly browned and knife inserted in centre comes out clean. Serve warm. Serves 8.

1 serving: 458 Calories; 15.9 g Total Fat (5.0 g Mono, 1.2 g Poly, 8.2 g Sat); 253 mg Cholesterol; 70 g Carbohydrate; 3 g Fibre; 12 g Protein; 163 mg Sodium

messy bed rhubarb dessert

Tuck rhubarb (or equal amounts of other cooked fruit) under crumpled sheets of phyllo for an easy, fun dessert that the kids will love—just don't let them hide the empty plates under their own messy beds!

Chopped fresh (or frozen, thawed) rhubarb	6 cups	1.5 L
Granulated sugar	1 cup	250 mL
Water	1/4 cup	60 mL
Grated orange zest	1 tsp.	5 mL
Ground cinnamon	1/2 tsp.	2 mL
Phyllo pastry sheets, thawed according to package directions	6	6
Cooking spray		
Icing (confectioner's) sugar	1 tsp.	5 mL

Combine first 5 ingredients in large saucepan. Bring to a boil on medium. Reduce heat to medium-low. Simmer, uncovered, for 12 to 15 minutes, stirring occasionally, until rhubarb starts to break up and sauce is thickened. Spread evenly in ungreased 9 inch (22 cm) deep dish pie plate.

Work with pastry sheets 1 at a time. Keep remaining sheets covered with damp tea towel to prevent drying. Spray 1 side of sheet with cooking spray. Loosely bunch. Place on top of rhubarb mixture near edge of pie plate. Spray second sheet with cooking spray. Loosely bunch. Place on top of rhubarb mixture, touching first sheet. Repeat with remaining sheets until rhubarb mixture is completely covered. Spray top of pastry with cooking spray. Bake in 350°F (175°C) oven for about 20 minutes until pastry is crisp and golden. Let stand for 10 minutes.

Sprinkle with icing sugar. Serve warm. Serves 6.

1 serving: 223 Calories; 1.4 g Total Fat (0.3 g Mono, 0.7 g Poly, 0.2 g Sat); 0 mg Cholesterol; 52 g Carbohydrate; 0 g Fibre; 3 g Protein; 149 mg Sodium

deep plum pie

You can substitute other plum varieties for the blue-toned prune plums. If you can't remove the waxed paper from the dough easily, throw it all into the freezer for a few minutes before trying again.

Fresh prune plums, halved and pitted	3 lbs.	1.4 kg
Granulated sugar	1 1/2 cups	375 mL
Minute tapioca	1/3 cup	75 mL
All-purpose flour	1 1/2 cups	375 mL
Salt	1/4 tsp.	1 mL
Butter (not margarine), chilled	1/2 cup	125 mL
Ice water	4 1/2 tbsp.	67 mL
Granulated sugar	2 tsp.	10 mL

Combine first 3 ingredients in large bowl. Transfer to greased 9 x 13 inch (22 x 33 cm) baking dish. Set aside.

Combine flour and salt in separate large bowl. Cut in butter until mixture resembles coarse crumbs.

Add ice water, 1 tbsp. (15 mL) at a time, stirring with fork until mixture starts to come together. Do not overmix. Turn out onto work surface. Shape into slightly flattened disc. Wrap with plastic wrap. Chill for 30 minutes. Roll out between 2 sheets of waxed paper to 10 x 14 inch (25 x 35 cm) rectangle. Remove top sheet of waxed paper. Turn, pastry side down, over plum mixture. Peel back waxed paper. Tuck into sides. Cut slits in top.

Sprinkle with second amount of sugar. Bake in 350°F (175°C) oven for about 1 hour until plum is soft and bubbling and crust is golden. Serve warm. Serves 12.

1 serving: 312 Calories; 9.0 g Total Fat (2.8 g Mono, 0.5 g Poly, 5.1 g Sat); 22 mg Cholesterol; 58 g Carbohydrate; 2 g Fibre; 3 g Protein; 133 mg Sodium

cherry nut crumble

The seeds of the nutmeg tree contain two spices: the actual nutmeg and the outer covering of the nutmeg, called mace. A nutmeg grater will allow you to really enjoy the fresh, aromatic flavour of this tropical spice.

Can of cherry pie filling	19 oz.	540 mL
Almond extract	1/4 tsp.	1 mL
Ground nutmeg	1/8 tsp.	0.5 mL
Brown sugar, packed	2/3 cup	150 mL
All-purpose flour	1/2 cup	125 mL
Quick-cooking rolled oats	1/2 cup	125 mL
Hard margarine (or butter), softened	6 tbsp.	100 mL
Sliced (or slivered) almonds	1/2 cup	125 mL

Combine first 3 ingredients in ungreased 2 quart (2 L) casserole.

Combine next 3 ingredients in medium bowl. Mix in margarine until mixture resembles coarse crumbs.

Add almonds. Stir. Sprinkle over cherry mixture. Bake in 350°F (175°C) oven for about 30 minutes until lightly browned. Let stand for 10 minutes before serving. Serve warm. Serves 6.

1 serving: 455 Calories; 18.5 g Total Fat (11.7 g Mono, 2.7 g Poly, 3.1 g Sat); 0 mg Cholesterol; 71 g Carbohydrate; 3 g Fibre; 5 g Protein; 156 mg Sodium

pear cranberry crumble

As a variation, leave out the pears and add 1 1/2 lbs. (680 g) fresh prune plums, pitted and sliced.

Peeled pears, cores removed and sliced	3	3
Bag of fresh (or frozen, thawed) cranberries	12 oz.	340 g
Brown sugar, packed	1/2 cup	125 mL
Minute tapioca	3 tbsp.	50 mL
Lemon juice	2 tsp.	10 mL
All-bran cereal	2/3 cup	150 mL
Quick-cooking rolled oats	2/3 cup	150 mL
Brown sugar, packed	1/3 cup	75 mL
Ground ginger	1/2 tsp.	2 mL
Ground cinnamon	1/4 tsp.	1 mL
Hard margarine (or butter), cut up	1/2 cup	125 mL

Vanilla ice cream (optional)

Combine first 5 ingredients in medium bowl. Spread evenly in greased shallow 2 quart (2 L) baking dish.

Combine next 5 ingredients in large bowl. Cut in margarine until mixture resembles coarse crumbs. Sprinkle evenly over pear mixture. Bake in 375ºF (190ºC) oven for 40 to 45 minutes until pear is tender and topping is browned. Let stand for 15 minutes.

Serve warm with ice cream. Serves 6.

1 serving: 397 Calories; 17.2 g Total Fat (10.7 g Mono, 1.9 g Poly, 3.5 g Sat); 0 mg Cholesterol; 63 g Carbohydrate; 8 g Fibre; 3 g Protein; 275 mg Sodium

blueberry cobbler

So named because the dropped dough looks like cobbled stones, this dish takes its place beside slumps, grunts, buckles and pandowdies as a tasty way to enjoy fruit desserts straight from the oven.

Hard margarine (or butter), melted	1/4 cup	60 mL
All-purpose flour	1 cup	250 mL
Milk	3/4 cup	175 mL
Granulated sugar	2 tbsp.	30 mL
Baking powder	2 tsp.	10 mL
Vanilla extract	1 tsp.	5 mL
Ground cinnamon	1/2 tsp.	2 mL
Ground nutmeg	1/4 tsp.	1 mL
Fresh (or frozen, thawed) blueberries	2 cups	500 mL
Granulated sugar	2 tbsp.	30 mL
Grated lemon zest	1 tsp.	5 mL
Water	1/2 cup	125 mL

Pour melted margarine into bottom of greased shallow baking dish. Set aside.

Combine next 7 ingredients in medium bowl. Drop by tablespoonfuls over margarine.

Combine next 3 ingredients in medium bowl. Sprinkle over flour mixture.

Drizzle with water. Do not stir. Bake in 350°F (175°C) oven for 40 to 45 minutes until bubbling and lightly browned. Serve warm. Serves 6.

1 serving: 232 Calories; 8.9 g Total Fat (5.4 g Mono, 0.9 g Poly, 1.9 g Sat); 1 mg Cholesterol; 35 g Carbohydrate; 2 g Fibre; 4 g Protein; 238 mg Sodium

rhubarb pinwheel cobbler

When neighbours leave rhubarb on your doorstep, chop it up and freeze in single layers on cookie sheets. Once frozen, it can be stored in freezer bags for desserts like this one!

Chopped fresh (or frozen, thawed) rhubarb	6 cups	1.5 L
Granulated sugar	1 1/2 cups	375 mL
Water	1/3 cup	75 mL
Minute tapioca	3 tbsp.	50 mL
Lemon juice (see Tip, page 64)	1 tbsp.	15 mL
All-purpose flour	2 cups	500 mL
Granulated sugar	1 1/2 tbsp.	25 mL
Baking powder	4 tsp.	20 mL
Salt	1/2 tsp.	2 mL
Milk	2/3 cup	150 mL
Cooking oil	3 tbsp.	50 mL
Hard margarine (or butter), melted	1 1/2 tsp.	7 mL
Grated lemon peel	1 tbsp.	15 mL
Granulated sugar	1/4 cup	60 mL

Combine first 5 ingredients in large saucepan. Heat, stirring occasionally, until boiling. Transfer to ungreased 3 quart (3 L) casserole. Bake, uncovered, in 450°F (230°C) oven for about 20 minutes.

Combine next 4 ingredients in medium bowl. Add milk and cooking oil. Stir until soft ball forms. Turn out onto lightly floured surface. Knead 8 times. Roll out to 1/2 inch (12 mm) thick rectangle about 10 inches (25 cm) long.

Brush melted margarine over surface.

Combine lemon peel and third amount of sugar in small cup. Sprinkle half over melted margarine. Roll up, jelly-roll style, from 10 inch (25 cm) side. Cut into 14 slices. Arrange over rhubarb, cut side down. Sprinkle with remaining lemon peel mixture. Bake for another 25 minutes. Serve warm. Serves 8.

1 serving: 404 Calories; 6.6 g Total Fat (3.6 g Mono, 1.8 g Poly, 0.7 g Sat); 1 mg Cholesterol; 83 g Carbohydrate; 3 g Fibre; 5 g Protein; 202 mg Sodium

pumpkin dessert

Almost like pumpkin pie—but without the crust. A cake mix makes this easy and fast—it takes only 20 minutes to assemble. Add a small dollop of ice cream for that delightful warm/cold contrast.

Large eggs	4	4
Granulated sugar	1 1/4 cups	300 mL
Cans of pure pumpkin (no spices), 14 oz., 398 mL, each	2	2
Ground cinnamon	1 1/2 tsp.	7 mL
Ground ginger	1 tsp.	5 mL
Salt	1 tsp.	5 mL
Ground cloves	1/2 tsp.	2 mL
Ground nutmeg	1/2 tsp.	2 mL
Evaporated milk (or half-and-half cream)	1 1/2 cups	375 mL
Box of yellow cake mix (2 layer size)	1	1
Hard margarine (or butter)	1/2 cup	125 mL
Vanilla ice cream (optional)		

Beat eggs in medium bowl until frothy. Add sugar. Beat until thick and pale.

Add next 6 ingredients. Beat well.

Add evaporated milk. Beat on low to blend. Pour into greased 9 x 13 inch (22 x 33 cm) pan.

Put cake mix into large bowl. Cut in margarine until mixture resembles coarse crumbs. Sprinkle over pumpkin mixture. Bake in 350°F (175°C) oven for 1 1/2 hours until knife inserted in centre comes out clean.

Serve warm with ice cream. Cuts into 18 squares.

1 serving: 266 Calories; 10.0 g Total Fat (7.5 g Mono, 1.1 g Poly, 2.8 g Sat); 58 mg Cholesterol; 41 g Carbohydrate; 1 g Fibre; 5 g Protein; 360 mg Sodium

pineapple nut kuchen

This kuchen (KOO-khen) is a not-too-sweet dessert that's easy on the waistline.

All-purpose flour	1/2 cup	125 mL
Yellow cornmeal	1/2 cup	125 mL
Quick-cooking rolled oats	1/3 cup	75 mL
Baking powder	1 tsp.	5 mL
Baking soda	1/8 tsp.	0.5 mL
Ground cinnamon	1/8 tsp.	0.5 mL
Large egg, fork-beaten	1	1
Non-fat plain yogurt	1/2 cup	125 mL
Brown sugar, packed	1/4 cup	60 mL
Margarine, melted	2 tbsp.	30 mL
Can of pineapple tidbits, drained	14 oz.	398 mL
Chopped pecans	2 tbsp.	30 mL
Liquid honey, warmed	2 tbsp.	30 mL

Combine first 6 ingredients in medium bowl.

Combine next 4 ingredients in small bowl. Add to dry ingredients. Stir until just moistened. Transfer to greased 9 inch (22 cm) glass pie plate.

Scatter pineapple and pecans over top. Lightly press with palm of hand. Drizzle with honey. Bake in 350°F (175°C) oven for 25 minutes until wooden pick inserted in centre comes out clean. Serve warm. Cuts into 8 wedges.

1 wedge: 188 Calories; 5.1 g Total Fat (2.9 g Mono, 0.9 g Poly, 0.9 g Sat); 27.2 mg Cholesterol; 32 g Carbohydrate; 2 g Fibre; 4 g Protein; 79 mg Sodium

maple apple fritters

The bubbles in the beer create the crisp, light batter for this tasty treat. What to do with the extra? That's the cook's reward!

MAPLE CREAM

Maple (or maple-flavoured) syrup	1/2 cup	125 mL
Sour cream	1/2 cup	125 mL
Brown sugar, packed	1/3 cup	75 mL
Whipping cream	1 cup	250 mL

APPLE FRITTERS

All-purpose flour	1 1/2 cups	375 mL
Granulated sugar	2 tbsp.	30 mL
Salt	1/4 tsp.	1 mL
Large eggs	2	2
Beer	1 cup	250 mL
Cooking oil	2 tbsp.	30 mL
Granulated sugar	1/3 cup	75 mL
Ground cinnamon	1/2 tsp.	2 mL
Large peeled tart apples (such as Granny Smith)	3	3
Cooking oil, for deep-frying		

Maple Cream: Combine first 3 ingredients in medium saucepan. Heat and stir on medium until brown sugar is dissolved. Bring to a gentle boil. Boil gently for 2 to 3 minutes, without stirring, until slightly thickened. Cool completely.

Beat whipping cream in medium bowl until soft peaks form. Add maple mixture. Stir. Chill, covered, until cold. Makes about 2 1/2 cups (625 mL) cream.

Apple Fritters: Combine first 3 ingredients in large bowl. Make a well in centre.

Add next 3 ingredients. Mix well. Let stand, covered, at room temperature for 2 hours.

Combine second amount of granulated sugar and cinnamon in small bowl.

Carefully remove cores from apples using apple corer, leaving apples whole. Cut into 1/3 inch (1 cm) slices. Dip individual slices into batter. Deep-fry, in batches, in hot (375°F, 190°C) cooking oil for about 2 minutes per batch until golden brown and crisp. Remove to paper towels to drain. Sprinkle with cinnamon mixture. Serve warm with Maple Cream. Makes about 32 fritters. Serves 8.

1 serving: 518 Calories; 26.6 g Total Fat (11.5 g Mono, 4.5 g Poly, 9.0 g Sat); 96 mg Cholesterol; 64 g Carbohydrate; 2 g Fibre; 5 g Protein; 116 mg Sodium

chocolate-studded dumplings

Chocolate chips decorate tasty morsels baked in a cocoa sauce. The sauce can be made ahead and reheated when you're ready to make the dumplings.

COCOA SAUCE

Water	1 3/4 cups	425 mL
Brown sugar, packed	1/2 cup	125 mL
Granulated sugar	1/2 cup	125 mL
All-purpose flour	2 tbsp.	30 mL
Cocoa, sifted if lumpy	2 tbsp.	30 mL
Hard margarine (or butter)	1 tbsp.	15 mL
Vanilla extract	1 tsp.	5 mL
Salt	1/4 tsp.	1 mL

DUMPLINGS

All-purpose flour	1 cup	250 mL
Semi-sweet chocolate chips	1/2 cup	125 mL
Granulated sugar	3 tbsp.	50 mL
Baking powder	1 1/2 tsp.	7 mL
Salt	1/2 tsp.	2 mL
Milk	1/2 cup	125 mL
Cooking oil	2 tbsp.	30 mL

Cocoa Sauce: Combine all 8 ingredients in small saucepan. Heat and stir on medium until boiling. Pour into ungreased 3 quart (3 L) casserole.

Dumplings: Combine first 5 ingredients in medium bowl. Add milk and cooking oil. Stir until soft dough forms. Drop by tablespoonfuls into Cocoa Sauce. Bake, uncovered, in 350°F (175°C) oven for about 30 minutes until wooden pick inserted in centre of dumpling comes out clean. Serve warm. Serves 8.

1 serving: 303 Calories; 9.4 g Total Fat (2.9 g Mono, 0.9 g Poly, 2.1 g Sat); trace Cholesterol; 54 g Carbohydrate; 1 g Fibre; 3 g Protein; 289 mg Sodium

warm 'n' saucy parcels

Crispy on the outside with softened fruit on the inside, these satisfying parcels are filling enough to help round out a light supper.

ORANGE SAUCE

Orange juice	2/3 cup	150 mL
Cornstarch	1 tbsp.	15 mL
Granulated sugar	1 tbsp.	15 mL
Grated orange zest	1/2 tsp.	2 mL
Orange liqueur	2 tbsp.	30 mL

PARCELS

Medium bananas, cut into 1/4 inch (6 mm) slices	2	2
Fresh (or frozen, thawed) blueberries	2/3 cup	150 mL
Whole-wheat flour tortillas (9 inch, 22 cm, diameter)	4	4
Non-fat vanilla (or blueberry) yogurt	3/4 cup	175 mL
Miniature marshmallows	2/3 cup	150 mL

Cooking spray
Ground cinnamon, sprinkle

Orange Sauce: Stir orange juice into cornstarch in small saucepan. Add sugar and zest. Heat and stir on medium until boiling and slightly thickened. Remove from heat.

Stir in liqueur. Makes about 3/4 cup (175 mL) sauce.

Parcels: Divide and arrange banana slices and blueberries down centre of tortillas.

Combine yogurt and marshmallows in small bowl. Spoon over fruit. Roll up tortillas, tucking in sides, to enclose filling. Arrange, seam-side down, on greased baking sheet.

Spray parcels with cooking spray. Sprinkle lightly with cinnamon. Bake in 425°F (220°C) oven for about 10 minutes until golden and crisp. Drizzle about 2 1/2 tbsp. (37 mL) sauce over each parcel. Serve warm. Makes 4 parcels.

1 parcel with sauce: 354 Calories; 2.2 g Total Fat (0.1 g Mono, 1.9 g Poly, 0.1 g Sat); 1 mg Cholesterol; 74 g Carbohydrate; 6 g Fibre; 8 g Protein; 429 mg Sodium

peach treasures

Packed inside layers of phyllo are delicious, golden peaches. For different treasures, omit the peaches and add two medium apples, peeled and sliced, and 1/3 cup (75 mL) chopped dried cranberries.

Chopped fresh (or frozen, thawed) peaches	2 cups	500 mL
Raisins	2 tbsp.	30 mL
Brown sugar, packed	1 tbsp.	15 mL
Lemon juice	1 tbsp.	15 mL
Minute tapioca	2 tsp.	10 mL
Ground cinnamon	1/2 tsp.	2 mL
Ground ginger	1/4 tsp.	1 mL
Fine dry whole-wheat bread crumbs (see Tip, page 64)	2 tbsp.	30 mL
Brown sugar, packed	1 1/2 tsp.	7 mL
Ground cinnamon	1/4 tsp.	1 mL
Phyllo pastry sheets, thawed according to package directions	12	12
Cooking spray		
Granulated sugar (optional)	1 tsp.	5 mL
Ground cinnamon, pinch (optional)		

Combine first 7 ingredients in medium bowl. Let stand for 10 minutes.

Combine next 3 ingredients in small bowl.

Work with pastry sheets 1 at a time. Keep remaining sheets covered with damp tea towel to prevent drying. Lay 1 pastry sheet on flat surface. Sprinkle with about 1 1/2 tsp. (7 mL) bread crumb mixture. Cover with second sheet. Fold in half widthwise. Spoon about 1/3 cup (75 mL) peach mixture 2 inches (5 cm) from narrow end, leaving 2 inches (5 cm) on either side. Roll edge over peach mixture. Fold in sides and continue rolling until filling is completely enclosed. Place seam-side down on greased baking sheet. Repeat with remaining ingredients.

Spray with cooking spray. Sprinkle with granulated sugar and cinnamon. Bake in 375°F (190°C) oven for about 20 minutes until golden brown. Serve warm. Makes 6 treasures.

1 treasure: 208 Calories; 1.2 g Total Fat (0.5 g Mono, 0.5 g Poly, 0.2 g Sat); trace Cholesterol; 46 g Carbohydrate; 2 g Fibre; 5 g Protein; 290 mg Sodium

baked stuffed apples

Few things are cosier than the scent of baked apples on a chilly evening.
The apples are scored to prevent them from looking "pruned" when
cooked. Cover the stuffing with foil to stop it from burning during the long
cooking time.

Brown sugar, packed	1/2 cup	125 mL
Coarsely chopped pecans, toasted (see Tip, page 64)	1/2 cup	125 mL
Golden raisins	1/2 cup	125 mL
Diced mixed peel	1/4 cup	60 mL
Hard margarine (or butter), softened	3 tbsp.	50 mL
Grated orange zest	2 tsp.	10 mL
Ground cinnamon	1/2 tsp.	2 mL
Large unpeeled tart apples (such as Granny Smith)	6	6
Apple juice	1/2 cup	125 mL

Combine first 7 ingredients in medium bowl.

Carefully remove cores from apples using apple corer, leaving apples
whole. Carefully cut around hole in each apple with knife to make hole
twice as large. Score peel of each apple vertically in several places. Arrange
apples in greased shallow 3 quart (3 L) baking dish. Spoon pecan mixture
into centre of each apple, piling excess on top. Cover exposed pecan
mixture with small pieces of foil.

Pour apple juice into baking dish around apples. Bake, uncovered, in 350°F
(175°C) oven for about 1 hour until apples are tender. Serve warm. Makes
6 stuffed apples.

1 stuffed apple: 350 Calories; 13.4 g Total Fat (8.2 g Mono, 2.5 g Poly, 1.9 g Sat);
0 mg Cholesterol; 61 g Carbohydrate; 5 g Fibre; 2 g Protein; 78 mg Sodium

brandied peaches

A dessert for all occasions. You can make the peaches a day ahead and gently reheat before serving.

Cans of peach halves in juice (14 oz., 398 mL, each), drained and juice reserved, chopped	2	2
Brown sugar, packed	2/3 cup	150 mL
Brandy	1/4 cup	60 mL
Butter (or hard margarine)	2 tbsp.	30 mL
Lemon juice	1 tsp.	5 mL
Ground cinnamon	1/4 tsp.	1 mL
Almond extract (optional)	1/4 tsp.	1 mL
Vanilla ice cream	6 cups	1.5 L

Combine first 7 ingredients in medium saucepan on medium. Bring to a boil. Reduce heat to medium-low. Simmer, uncovered, for 5 minutes, stirring occasionally.

Scoop about 1/2 cup (125 mL) ice cream into 12 bowls. Spoon warm Brandied Peaches over top. Serves 12.

1 serving: 373 Calories; 19.9 g Total Fat (0.5 g Mono, 0.1 g Poly, 12.1 g Sat); 125 mg Cholesterol; 41 g Carbohydrate; 1 g Fibre; 5 g Protein; 91 mg Sodium

banana flambé

Choose bananas with skins that haven't started to turn brown. These are fabulous over frozen vanilla yogurt, or as a filling for crepes.

Butter (or hard margarine)	1/4 cup	60 mL
Brown sugar, packed	1/2 cup	125 mL
Ground cinnamon	1/2 tsp.	2 mL
Whipping cream	1/4 cup	60 mL
Firm medium bananas, cut into 1 inch (2.5 cm) pieces	3	3
Amber (golden) or dark (navy) rum	1/3 cup	75 mL
Banana liqueur	1/4 cup	60 mL

Melt butter in large frying pan on medium. Add brown sugar and cinnamon. Heat and stir for about 3 minutes until bubbling and brown sugar is dissolved.

Add whipping cream. Stir.

Add banana. Stir until coated. Remove from heat.

Heat rum and liqueur in small saucepan on medium until hot. Carefully pour over banana mixture in frying pan. Heat on medium, shaking pan back and forth 2 or 3 times. Carefully ignite surface with match. Gently swirl pan several times until flames subside. Spoon sauce over banana until coated. Makes about 2 1/2 cups (625 mL). Serve warm. Serves 6.

1 serving: 305 Calories; 11.9 g Total Fat (3.4 g Mono, 0.5 g Poly, 7.3 g Sat); 34 mg Cholesterol; 38 g Carbohydrate; 1 g Fibre; 1 g Protein; 96 mg Sodium

poached maple pears

Port wine is a fortified red or white wine originally developed in Portugal. Choose red port for this recipe, as it gives the pears their wonderful ruby colour in this elegant, virtually no-fat dessert.

Firm peeled pears	4	4
Port wine	1 cup	250 mL
Orange juice	1/2 cup	125 mL
Maple (or maple-flavoured) syrup	1/3 cup	75 mL
Cinnamon stick (4 inches, 10 cm)	1	1
Whole cloves	6	6

Fresh mint leaves, for garnish

Carefully remove cores from pears using apple corer, leaving pears whole.

Combine next 5 ingredients in medium saucepan. Lay pears on sides in wine mixture. Bring to a boil on medium. Reduce heat to medium-low. Simmer, uncovered, for 15 to 20 minutes, turning occasionally, until softened and evenly coloured. Remove pears using slotted spoon. Cover to keep warm. Remove and discard cinnamon stick and cloves. Bring wine mixture to a boil on medium. Boil, uncovered, for 10 to 15 minutes until reduced to about 3/4 cup (175 mL).

Slice pears evenly, making 6 or 7 cuts from large end of pear to within 1/2 inch (12 mm) of small end. Place 1 pear, large end down, on each of 4 dessert plates. Fan pear slices out slightly. Drizzle with wine mixture. Garnish with mint leaves. Serve warm. Serves 4.

1 serving: 177 Calories; 0.2 g Total Fat (0 g Mono, 0 g Poly, 0 g Sat); 0 mg Cholesterol; 35 g Carbohydrate; 3 g Fibre; 1 g Protein; 9 mg Sodium

spiced mango pears

Assemble the pears ahead of time, then bake as directed while you're enjoying your entree. Try freshly squeezed orange juice for a burst of tangy flavour in the sauce, which can be kept sealed and chilled for five days.

Can of sliced mango in syrup, drained and syrup reserved, chopped	14 oz.	398 mL
Grated lime zest	1 tsp.	5 mL
Ground cinnamon	1/4 tsp.	1 mL
Ground cardamom	1/8 tsp.	0.5 mL
Reserved mango syrup		
Lime juice	1 tbsp.	15 mL
Can of pear halves in light syrup, drained	28 oz.	796 mL
Chopped pistachios	1/4 cup	60 mL
Brown sugar, packed	2 tbsp.	30 mL

RASPBERRY LIQUEUR SAUCE

Container of frozen raspberries in syrup, thawed	15 oz.	425 g
Raspberry liqueur	2 tbsp.	30 mL
Cornstarch	1 tbsp.	15 mL
Orange juice	1/4 cup	60 mL

Combine first 4 ingredients in medium bowl.

Combine reserved mango syrup and lime juice in ungreased 9 inch (22 cm) deep-dish pie plate. Arrange pear halves, cut-side up, over syrup mixture. Spoon mango mixture into centre of pear halves.

Sprinkle pistachios and brown sugar over mango mixture. Bake in 375°F (190°C) oven for about 15 minutes until heated through and pistachios are toasted. Serve warm. Serves 6.

Raspberry Liqueur Sauce: Press raspberries with syrup through sieve into medium saucepan. Bring to a boil. Reduce heat to medium.

Stir liqueur into cornstarch in small cup until smooth. Add to raspberry mixture. Heat and stir for about 1 minute until boiling and thickened. Remove from heat.

Add orange juice. Stir. Cool. Makes about 1 1/2 cups (375 mL) sauce. Serve with warm pears. Serves 6.

1 serving: 217 Calories; 3.1 g Total Fat (1.9 g Mono, 0.6 g Poly, 0.4 g Sat); 0 mg Cholesterol; 46 g Carbohydrate; 7 g Fibre; 3 g Protein; 8 mg Sodium

chocolate silk fondue

Spectacularly easy, but so smooth, warm and delicious! Choose good-quality chocolate and add a splash of your favourite liqueur if this is an all-adult treat. Try ladyfingers, cubes of angel food or pound cake and bite-sized pieces of fruit as dipping options.

Dark chocolate bars	2	2
(3 1/2 oz., 100 g, each), chopped		
Whipping cream	1 cup	250 mL

Heat chocolate and whipping cream in small heavy saucepan on lowest heat, stirring often until chocolate is almost melted. Do not overheat. Remove from heat. Stir until smooth. Pour into fondue pot. Keep warm over low flame. Serve with your choice of dippers. Makes about 1 2/3 cups (400 mL) fondue.

2 tbsp. (30 mL): 124 Calories; 10.1 g Total Fat (3.1 g Mono, 0.3 g Poly, 6.2 g Sat); 21 mg Cholesterol; 10 g Carbohydrate; 1 g Fibre; 1 g Protein; 8 mg Sodium

backwards fondue

The chocolate is in the dippers, not the fondue! Surround your fondue with cocoa-flavoured morsels such as cubed chocolate pound cake, doughnuts, loaf cake and fruit cake.

Brown sugar, packed	2 cups	500 mL
Can of sweetened condensed milk	11 oz.	300 mL
Dark corn syrup	3/4 cup	175 mL
Hard margarine (or butter)	1/4 cup	60 mL
Water	2 tbsp.	30 mL
Vanilla extract	1 tsp.	5 mL

Combine all 6 ingredients in medium heavy saucepan. Heat and stir on low for about 10 minutes until thickened. Pour into fondue pot. Keep warm over low flame. Serve with your choice of dippers. Makes about 2 3/4 cups (675 mL) fondue.

2 tbsp. (30 mL): 183 Calories; 3.6 g Total Fat (1.8 g Mono, 0.3 g Poly, 1.4 g Sat); 6 mg Cholesterol; 37 g Carbohydrate; trace Fibre; 1 g Protein; 61 mg Sodium

eggnog fondue

Over the holidays, try fruitcake as a dipper for this festive version of fondue. Other dippers to use include angel food or chocolate cake cubes, soft ginger cookies, doughnut pieces and bite-sized chunks of fruit.

All-purpose flour	2 tbsp.	30 mL
Cornstarch	2 tbsp.	30 mL
Brown sugar, packed	1 tbsp.	15 mL
Salt, just a pinch		
Eggnog	2 cups	500 mL
Milk	1 cup	250 mL
Large egg, fork-beaten	1	1
Vanilla extract	1 tsp.	5 mL
Ground cinnamon, sprinkle		
Ground nutmeg, sprinkle		
Dark (navy) rum	2 tbsp.	30 mL

Combine first 4 ingredients in large saucepan.

Slowly stir in eggnog and milk until smooth. Heat and stir on medium until boiling and slightly thickened. Remove from heat.

Combine next 4 ingredients in small bowl. Add 1 tbsp. (15 mL) hot eggnog mixture to egg mixture. Stir. Add egg mixture to remaining hot eggnog mixture. Heat and stir on medium-low for 2 minutes. Remove from heat.

Add rum. Stir. Pour into fondue pot. Keep warm over low flame. Add eggnog or rum as necessary for desired dipping consistency. Serve with your choice of dippers. Makes about 3 cups (750 mL) fondue.

__2 tbsp. (30 mL):__ 46 Calories; 1.9 g Total Fat (0.6 g Mono, 0.1 g Poly, 1.1 g Sat); 22 mg Cholesterol; 5 g Carbohydrate; trace Fibre; 1 g Protein; 20 mg Sodium

chocolate hazelnut soufflés

A hint of hazelnut liqueur flavours these chocolate soufflés. For best results, serve this light, fluffy dessert immediately.

Granulated sugar	1 tbsp.	15 mL
Butter (or hard margarine)	2 tbsp.	30 mL
All-purpose flour	2 tbsp.	30 mL
Hazelnut liqueur	1/4 cup	60 mL
Milk	3 tbsp.	50 mL
Semi-sweet chocolate baking squares (1 oz., 28 g, each), chopped	3	3
Egg yolks (large), fork-beaten	3	3
Granulated sugar	3 tbsp.	50 mL
Egg whites (large), room temperature	3	3

Cocoa, for dusting

Sprinkle first amount of sugar into greased 1/2 cup (125 mL) ramekin. Tilt ramekin to coat bottom and side with sugar. Gently tap excess sugar into another greased ramekin. Repeat 3 more times for a total of 4 sugar-coated ramekins. Place ramekins on baking sheet with sides. Set aside.

Melt butter in small saucepan on medium. Add flour. Heat and stir for about 1 minute until bubbling. Slowly add liqueur and milk, stirring constantly, until smooth.

Add chocolate. Heat and stir until chocolate is almost melted. Remove from heat. Stir until smooth.

Add egg yolks and second amount of sugar. Stir. Transfer to large bowl.

Beat egg whites in medium bowl until soft peaks form. Fold about 1/3 of egg whites into chocolate mixture until almost combined. Fold chocolate mixture into remaining egg whites until just combined (see Tip, page 64). Spoon into prepared ramekins. Smooth tops. Run thumb around inside edge of ramekins in soufflé mixture to ensure even rising during baking (see inset photo). Bake in 375°F (190°C) oven for 12 to 15 minutes, without opening oven door, until very puffed.

Dust with cocoa using a sieve. Serve immediately. Serves 4.

1 serving: 337 Calories; 16.6 g Total Fat (5.4 g Mono, 1.0 g Poly, 8.9 g Sat); 179 mg Cholesterol; 36 g Carbohydrate; 1 g Fibre; 6 g Protein; 121 mg Sodium

orange soufflé clouds

These individual soufflés will have you feeling lighter than air. The inset photo on the previous page illustrates how to run your thumb inside the ramekin to create perfect soufflés.

Granulated sugar	2 tbsp.	30 mL
Skim milk	1 cup	250 mL
Cornstarch	2 tbsp.	30 mL
Granulated sugar	3 tbsp.	50 mL
Egg yolk (large), fork-beaten	1	1
Orange juice (see Tip, page 64)	1/3 cup	75 mL
Grated orange zest	1 tbsp.	15 mL
Egg whites (large), room temperature	5	5
Cream of tartar	1/2 tsp.	2 mL
Granulated sugar	3 tbsp.	50 mL

Sprinkle first amount of sugar into greased 6 oz. (170 mL) ramekin. Tilt ramekin to coat bottom and side with sugar. Gently tap excess sugar into another greased ramekin. Repeat 5 more times for a total of 6 sugar-coated ramekins. Place ramekins on baking sheet with sides. Set aside.

Stir milk into cornstarch in small saucepan. Add second amount of sugar. Heat and stir on medium for about 5 minutes until boiling and thickened.

Combine next 3 ingredients in small cup. Add to milk mixture, stirring constantly with whisk for about 1 minute until thickened. Transfer to medium bowl.

Beat egg whites and cream of tartar in large bowl until soft peaks form. Add third amount of sugar, 1 tbsp. (15 mL) at a time, beating constantly until stiff peaks form and sugar is dissolved. Fold about 1/3 of egg white mixture into hot milk mixture until almost combined. Fold milk mixture into remaining egg whites until just combined (see Tip, page 64). Spoon into ramekins. Smooth tops. Run thumb around inside edge of ramekins in soufflé mixture to ensure even rising during baking (see inset photo, page 59). Bake in 400°F (205°C) oven for about 12 minutes, without opening oven door, until very puffed and tops are golden. Serve immediately. Serves 6.

1 serving: 115 Calories; 1.0 g Total Fat (0.4 g Mono, 0.1 g Poly, 0.3 g Sat); 32 mg Cholesterol; 22 g Carbohydrate; trace Fibre; 5 g Protein; 68 mg Sodium

recipe index

topical tips

Bruising cardamom: To release the flavour of this fragrant spice, pound pods with a mallet or press with flat side of a wide knife to "bruise," or crack them open slightly.

Folding in egg whites for soufflés: This is a crucial factor in making well-risen soufflés. Use a metal spoon with a thin edge to fold in the egg whites. It won't deflate the air bubbles in the mixture in the same way a thick wooden spoon will. Use a light touch and don't overmix.

Making bread crumbs: To make 1/4 cup (60 mL) dry whole-wheat bread crumbs, remove the crusts from one slice of stale one or two-day-old whole-wheat bread. Leave the bread on the counter for a day or two until it's dry, or, if you're in a hurry, set the bread on a baking sheet and bake in a 200°F (95°C) oven or toaster oven, turning occasionally, until dry. Break the bread into pieces and process until crumbs reach the desired fineness.

Toasting nuts, seeds or coconut: Cooking times will vary for each type of nut, so never toast them together. For small amounts, place ingredient in an ungreased shallow frying pan. Heat on medium for three to five minutes, stirring often, until golden. For larger amounts, spread ingredient evenly in an ungreased shallow pan. Bake in a 350°F (175°C) oven for five to 10 minutes, stirring or shaking often, until golden.

Zest first; juice second: When a recipe calls for grated zest and juice, it's easier to grate the lemon or lime first, then juice it. Be careful not to grate down to the pith (white part of the peel), which is bitter and best avoided.

Nutrition Information Guidelines

Each recipe is analyzed using the Canadian Nutrient File from Health Canada, which is based on the United States Department of Agriculture (USDA) Nutrient Database.

- If more than one ingredient is listed (such as "butter or hard margarine"), or if a range is given (1 – 2 tsp., 5 – 10 mL), only the first ingredient or first amount is analyzed.

- For meat, poultry and fish, the serving size per person is based on the recommended 4 oz. (113 g) uncooked weight (without bone), which is 2 – 3 oz. (57 – 85 g) cooked weight (without bone) — approximately the size of a deck of playing cards.

- Milk used is 1% M.F. (milk fat), unless otherwise stated.

- Cooking oil used is canola oil, unless otherwise stated.

- Ingredients indicating "sprinkle," "optional" or "for garnish" are not included in the nutrition information.

- The fat in recipes and combination foods can vary greatly depending on the sources and types of fats used in each specific ingredient. For these reasons, the count of saturated, monounsaturated and polyunsaturated fats may not add up to the total fat content.